OVERFLOWING WITH THE HOLY SPIRIT

KNOW THE PERSON OF THE HOLY SPIRIT AND LEARN TO WALK IN HIS POWER

Overflowing with the Holy Spirit

Know the Person of the Holy Spirit
and Learn To Walk in His Power

by

Pat Harrison

HARRISON HOUSE

Tulsa, Oklahoma

2nd Printing

Overflowing with the Holy Spirit
Know the Person of the Holy Spirit
and Learn To Walk in His Power
(revised from the book *Learning the Ways*
of the Holy Spirit 0-89274-564-9)
ISBN 1-57794-128-4
Copyright © 1998 by Pat Harrison
P. O. Box 35443
Tulsa, Oklahoma 74153

Published by Harrison House, Inc.
P. O. Box 35035
Tulsa, Oklahoma 74153

Contents

Contents

Introduction

These are serious days for the Body of Christ and for us as individuals. The clock is ticking steadily toward the turn of a new century *and* toward the time when our Lord will return for His Church. I am convinced that now more than ever the Body of Christ must mature in the ways of the Holy Spirit in order to fulfill God's plan and purpose for His Kingdom.

As I travel and teach in churches and conferences, it is evident to me that despite the awakening and fresh wave of the Holy Spirit we are seeing and experiencing, many Christians still do not know how to walk in holiness or how to appropriate the power of the Holy Spirit in their daily walk.

As sin abounds and as the kingdom of darkness wages its final battles, it is time to destroy the lies and deceptions Satan has used to confuse and separate the Body of Christ on this subject. The only way we are going to fulfill the Commission Jesus left with us is to have *both* the indwelling presence of the Holy Spirit and His power and might fully operating in our lives. The problem is most believers don't know the difference between the two or how to walk forth in the fullness of all that God has called them to do.

In my previous book, *Learning the Ways of the Holy Spirit,* I shared a very concise and simple explanation of the functions of the Holy Spirit, the working of the Holy Spirit within, how to learn the ways of the Holy Spirit and how to be perfected by the Holy Spirit. After teaching this material for the past nine years, it is now time to take this teaching up another level.

In this new book, *Overflowing with the Holy Spirit,* I have shared the expanded wisdom and revelation the Lord has imparted to me to bring greater growth and maturity to the Body of Christ through the Spirit of Truth and the enlightenment of the Word.

When you come into the kingdom of God by receiving Jesus as your Savior, the Holy Spirit indwells you with His presence. This indwelling is to benefit you as an individual to help you learn to walk in holiness and oneness with the Lord Jesus Christ. You have a part to play in this process in that you must *allow* the Holy Spirit to work on the inside of you.

We look at Jesus Christ to see what we ought to be, and we look to the Holy Spirit to make us what we ought to be. It is the indwelling Holy Spirit that brings the nine fruits of the Spirit to maturity in our recreated human spirits so we learn to walk in the righteousness of Christ on the earth in God's plan of salvation. The fruit of the Spirit will mature in us and that fruit will be seen because we are alive in God. It is through that vine that our branches bloom with fruit.

Once we are established in the indwelling of the Holy Spirit, the fullness causes an overflow, the outpouring, that reaches out to others. The outpouring of the Holy Spirit is for the benefit of others to bring them into the fullness of the Holy Spirit. In other words, the work of the Holy Spirit dwelling in us is to renew us continually so that the power can come forth to manifest as the Spirit wills to bless others.

First the Indwelling Then the Outpouring

ᔕ ᔕ ᔕ

When we receive Jesus as our Savior by asking Him into our hearts and confessing Him as Lord, the Holy Spirit comes to live inside us — to indwell us through the new birth. Not only that, the Holy Spirit woos us into the new birth. First Corinthians 12:3 AMP tells us we cannot even call Jesus Lord except by the Holy Spirit.

> **Therefore I want you to understand that no one speaking under the power *and* influence of the [Holy] Spirit of God can [ever] say, Jesus be cursed! And no one can [really] say, Jesus is [my] Lord, except by *and* under the power *and* influence of the Holy Spirit.**

Why is that? It is because the Holy Spirit is the One that draws us to Jesus. The Holy Spirit is the One that is doing the work in this earth through the believer because Jesus is no longer on the earth in Person.

> **And I [Jesus] will ask the Father, and He will give you another Comforter (Counselor, Helper, Intercessor, Advocate, Strengthener, and Standby), that He may remain with you forever, The Spirit of**

Truth, Whom the world cannot receive (welcome, take to its heart), because it does not see Him or know *and* recognize Him. But you know *and* recognize Him, for He lives with you [constantly] and will be in you.

John 14:16-17 AMP

In this Scripture, Jesus said He was not going to leave us comfortless and helpless when He went back to His Father. He said He was leaving Someone here on this earth to dwell in us forever who will help bring His Word to pass. That Someone is the Holy Spirit. He comes to indwell us, and it is through that indwelling presence that we, individually, allow the Holy Spirit to work in us and accomplish God's purpose in us. The maturing, perfecting, growing, under-standing, knowledge and wisdom we receive comes from the indwelling presence within us of the Holy Spirit. In other words, the indwelling presence of the Holy Spirit is to benefit the individual.

And then when we receive the fullness or infilling of the Holy Spirit with speaking in tongues, there is power that comes upon us — an outpouring — so we not only have the indwelling presence, but we have the power to fulfill the Commission Jesus left with us.

But you shall receive power — ability, efficiency, and might — when the Holy Spirit has come upon you, and you shall be My witnesses in Jerusalem and all Judea and Samaria and to the ends — the very bounds — of the earth.

Acts 1:8 AMP

Through the infilling or fullness of walking in the Holy Spirit — learning to yield ourselves to the Holy Spirit, to speak in tongues, and to pray in the Spirit that perfect prayer one for another — we are empowered to reach out and bless others. The indwelling is for the individual, and the outpouring or the endowment of power is to benefit or bless others.

When we delve into this a little further in the book, you will see how in some areas we have tried to work this backwards. I want to stress the difference between the indwelling and the outpouring or endowment of power. You can be witnesses of the "born again experience" spoken of by Jesus in Acts 1:8 through the indwelling of the Holy Spirit. But you can't be a witness to His power and all the things that come along with that power until you have experienced it by receiving the Holy Spirit in His fullness. It is important to understand the difference.

DRINK FROM THE WELL OF LIVING WATER

§ § §

To establish ourselves in the fact that there is an indwelling of the Holy Spirit, let's look at the story of the woman who met Jesus at the well outside a city in Samaria.

> **And in doing so, He arrived at a Samaritan town called Sychar, near the tract of land that Jacob gave to his son Joseph. And Jacob's well was there. So Jesus, tired as He was from His journey, sat down [to rest] by the well. It was about the sixth hour (about noon). Presently, when a woman of Samaria came along to draw water, Jesus said to**

11

her, Give Me a drink. For His disciples had gone off into the town to buy food. The Samaritan woman said to Him, How is it that You, being a Jew, ask me, a Samaritan [and a] woman, for a drink? For the Jews have nothing to do with the Samaritans. Jesus answered her, If you had only known and had recognized God's gift and Who this is that is saying to you, Give Me a drink, you would have asked Him instead and He would have given you living water.

She said to Him, Sir, You have nothing to draw with [no drawing bucket] and the well is deep; how then can You provide living water? — Where do You get Your living water? Are You greater than and superior to our ancestor Jacob, who gave us this well and who used to drink from it himself, and his sons and his cattle also?

Jesus answered her, All who drink of this water will be thirsty again. But whoever takes a drink of the water that I will give him shall never, no never, be thirsty any more. But the water that I will give him shall become a spring of water welling up (flowing, bubbling) continually within him unto (into, for) eternal life.

John 4:5-14 AMP

So what was Jesus saying to this woman? He was saying to her and to us, "When you receive Me, there is a well of water than begins to spring up within your spirit that causes you never to be thirsty. As you continually live within the realm of the Spirit because I am on the inside of you, you can draw from My well every day." In this passage, the well represents the Holy Spirit that dwells within us to benefit us continually if we allow it. The reason we sometimes become dry and thirsty for the things of God is that we do not keep that continual well of fellowship with Him bubbling up within us.

All through the Word we see that water is a type of the Holy Spirit. Jesus speaks again of this living water in John 7:37-39 AMP.

> ...If any man is thirsty, let him come to Me and drink! He who believes in Me — who cleaves to *and* trusts in *and* relies on Me — as the Scripture has said, out from his innermost being springs and rivers of living water shall flow (continuously).
>
> But He was speaking here of the Spirit, Whom those who believed — trusted, had faith — in Him were afterward to receive. For the [Holy] Spirit had not yet been given; because Jesus was not yet glorified (raised to honor).

The well, the spring, that is continually springing up within you is for you, but the river flowing out is to bless others. And it is important to have both operating in your life.

The indwelling of the Holy Spirit is also referred to by using the term "spirit of adoption." Galatians 4:4-7 AMP states:

> But when the proper time had fully come, God sent His Son, born of a woman, born subject to [the regulations of] the Law, To purchase the freedom of (to ransom, to redeem, to atone for) those who were subject to the Law, that we be adopted and have sonship conferred upon us [and

13

be recognized as God's sons]. **And because you
[really] are [His] sons, God has sent the [Holy]
Spirit of His Son into our hearts, crying, Abba
(Father)! Father! Therefore, you are no longer a
slave (bond servant) but a son; and if a son, then
[it follows that you are] an heir by the aid of God,
through Christ.**

So what God is saying to us here is through coming into
the family of God, He adopts us. We are adopted into the
kingdom of God, and we have sonship conferred upon us
through Jesus Christ. He is the first Son, and then there are
many sons through Christ Jesus because everything God
does He multiplies. So everything He does in your life is
going to multiply, if you allow it to happen through the Holy
Spirit, through His indwelling presence.

GOD WANTS YOU!

ʂ   ʂ   ʂ

John 1:12 says:

> **But as many as received him, to them gave he
> power to become the sons of God, even to them
> that believe on his name.**

If you just believe on His name, you obtain the right to
become a son through Jesus. You don't have to wonder if
God wanted you. You don't have to wonder if you are going
to be in the right place at the right time because you are in
the kingdom of God. You know that because God gave His
Son, and He adopted you into His family — He wanted you!
When a couple adopts a child in the natural, they don't just
do it to be nice. They do it because they want a child. Well,

God gave the very best He had — His Son — to us because He wanted us. He wanted you!

Through that spirit of adoption, that indwelling presence of the Spirit of God, you can be what Jesus, and really the Father God, desires you to be — a friend to Him, in fellowship with Him, having intimate relationship with Him — because the Holy Spirit is in you, and He knows the Father. You will know the Father by the Spirit of God and the Word of God.

There are people who do not have the fullness of the Holy Spirit with speaking in tongues, but they know the Spirit of God. And how much more should we, people who consider ourselves Holy Ghost "Word" people, have the well of life continually springing up within us instead of long, sad faces? What kind of Christian witness is that? The people in the world do not want that — they already have that! They are looking for life — *living water*.

The New Testament talks about the joy a believer can have — great joy.

Then He conducted them out as far as Bethany, and, lifting up His hands, He invoked a blessing on them. And it occurred that while He was blessing them, He parted from them and was taken up into heaven. And they, worshipping Him, went back to Jerusalem with great joy; And they were continually in the temple *celebrating with praises and* **blessing** *and* **extolling God. Amen (so be it).**

Luke 24:50-53 AMP

One of the fruits of the indwelling Holy Spirit is joy. When you have the joy of the Lord and you are operating in it, you have a smile on your face and a light shining from you. That joy attracts believers. Unbelievers understand happiness, but they know that they cannot remain happy because circumstances are not always happy. They desire to be joyful, to be full of something that causes them at all times to remain joyous.

The Infilling of the Holy Spirit
Is the Door to the Outpouring

ᚠ   ᚠ   ᚠ

It is by the fullness of the Spirit of God and that overflowing of the enduing of power that causes you to reach out and bring someone else into the fullness of the Holy Spirit. That well of living water inside you becomes a river that pours out to bless others. The infilling of the Holy Spirit is the door into the fullness of walking in the nine manifestations of the Spirit.

It is by the Spirit of God that you rise up and, according to Matthew 17:20, speak to the mountain of need in someone's life and tell it to be removed.

If ye have faith as a grain of mustard seed, ye shall say unto this mountain, Remove hence to yonder place; and it shall remove; and nothing shall be impossible unto you.

It is by the Spirit of God that you speak to that person who is not well and say, "Be healed in the name of Jesus!" It is by the Spirit of God that you speak to the enemy, Satan, and tell him that he will not prevail in someone's life — that only truth will prevail.

Signs and wonders follow those who believe as it says in Mark 16:17,18.

> **And these signs and wonders shall follow them that believe; In my name shall they cast out devils; they shall speak with new tongues; They shall take up serpents; and if they drink any deadly thing, it shall not hurt them; they shall lay hands on the sick, and they shall recover.**

We should not go out seeking signs and wonders, but seeking Jesus. If we concentrate on developing the fullness of the Holy Spirit inside us, in the outpouring, the signs and wonders will come.

The reason that the power of the Holy Spirit is not fully operational in the Body of Christ today is not because God has not done what He said He would do in the Bible. The reason is that believers have not done what God told us to do — to know the Spirit of God. We cannot have the power of the Holy Spirit operating in us when we do not know Him.

Perhaps you are a child of God and you are born of the Spirit of God, but you have not experienced the fullness of the Holy Spirit — being "filled" with the Spirit with evidence of speaking in tongues. If you are not familiar with what I mean by that, I will explain. When I say "filled," I mean what Acts 2:4 says, **And they were all filled with the Holy Ghost, and began to speak with other tongues, as the Spirit gave them utterance.**

If you want to experience this fullness by receiving the gift of the Holy Spirit, just pray and ask the Father God to give this to you. Believe that you have received the Holy Spirit. Now you should have a desire to speak words of a language other than your own. Lift your voice and begin to speak those words of that other language to God.

CHAPTER 2

⑨ ──────────────────────────────── ⑨

What Did Jesus Do?

⑨ ⑨ ⑨

There is a popular saying being used in Christian circles today, "What Would Jesus Do?" or "W.W.J.D." It appears on bracelets, hats, tee shirts and other items as a witnessing tool and also as a reminder for people to consider that question before they make hasty decisions or choices in life. But before we can even think about what Jesus *would* do in a situation, we need to know "What Jesus *Did* Do!" We need to have a clear understanding of the meaning of the Cross and the purpose for which Jesus left the Holy Spirit with us when He went back to the Father.

A NEW COVENANT

⑨ ⑨ ⑨

The Scriptures tell us that God has given us what we need to live in the fullness of the Spirit. He made a new convenant with us, but we have to abide in that covenant. Look at Hebrews 8:7-10 AMP:

> **For if that first covenant had been without defect, there would have been no room for another one or an attempt to institute another one.**

19

However, He finds fault with them [showing its inadequacy] when He says, Behold, the days will come, says the Lord, when I will make *and* ratify a new covenant *or* agreement with the house of Israel and with the house of Judah.

It will not be like the covenant that I made with their forefathers on the day when I grasped them by the hand to help *and* relieve them *and* to lead them out from the land of Egypt, for they did not abide in My agreement with them, and so I withdrew My favor *and* disregarded them, says the Lord.

For this is the covenant that I will make with the house of Israel after those days, says the Lord: I will imprint My laws upon their minds, even upon their innermost thoughts and understanding, and engrave them upon thoughts, and we can live with an established heart unto God.

God prophesied what He would do for us through Jesus in Ezekiel and Jeremiah. Again we see reference to the cleansing water of the Holy Spirit and of the indwelling of His Spirit in us.

Then will I sprinkle clean water upon you, and you shall be clean from all your uncleanness; and from all your idols will I cleanse you. A new heart will I give you, and a new spirit will I put within you: and I will take away the stony heart out of your flesh and give you a heart of flesh. And I will put my Spirit within you and cause you to walk in My statutes, and you shall heed My ordinances, and do them.

Ezekiel 36:25-27 AMP

> But this is the covenant which I will make with the house of Israel: After those days, says the Lord, I will put My law within them, and on their hearts will I write it; and I will be their God, and they will be My people. And they will no more teach each man his neighbor and each man his brother, saying, Know the Lord, for they will all know Me — recognize, understand, and be acquainted with Me — from the least of them to the greatest, says the Lord. For I will forgive their iniquity, and I will [seriously] remember their sin no more.
>
> **Jeremiah 31:33-34 AMP**

He is saying that as we operate in this new covenant, He will give us a new heart, and His Spirit will indwell us, causing us to walk in the truth of the Word and do it. He will be our God, and we will be His people.

CREATED IN HIS IMAGE

§ § §

God created us in His image for a purpose.

> God said, Let Us [Father, Son, and Holy Spirit] make mankind in Our image, after Our likeness, and let them have complete authority over the fish of the sea, the birds of the air, the [tame] beasts, and over all of the earth, and over everything that creeps upon the earth. So God created man in His own image, in the image and likeness of God He created him; male and female He created them.
>
> **Genesis 1:26-27 AMP**

God created man in His image so that He could relate to man, and man could relate to Him. The very first purpose for creating man was for fellowship with Him. Therefore, we had to be created in His image so that we could relate and fellowship with Him — spirit to Spirit. After all, the animals couldn't relate to or fellowship with God because they don't have a spirit. Man does and that is what makes us like God because God is a Spirit.

God is a Spirit (a spiritual Being) and those who worship Him must worship Him in spirit and in truth (reality).

John 4:24 AMP

The Holy Spirit brings that truth to us in revelation and understanding, and when we have understanding, we can operate in the wisdom of that knowledge which comes through the Holy Spirit.

THE FINAL SACRIFICE

֍ ֍ ֍

Now let's look more closely at what Jesus really did. We already read in Jeremiah 31:34 that part of the New Covenant would provide complete forgiveness of sins. Jesus made Himself a sacrifice so that once and for all our sins would be forgiven. This negated the need for continual daily sacrifices which had been made by the priests under the Old Covenant. In Hebrews 10:12-23 AMP we can read the rest of the story.

Whereas this One (Christ), after He had offered a single sacrifice for our sins [that shall avail] for all time, sat down at the right hand of God, Then to

22

wait until His enemies should be made a stool beneath His feet. For by a single offering He has forever completely cleansed *and* perfected those who are consecrated and made holy.

And also the Holy Spirit adds His testimony to us [in confirmation of this]. For having said, This is the agreement (testament, covenant) that I will set up *and* conclude with them after those days, says the Lord: I will imprint My laws upon their hearts, and I will inscribe them on their minds — on their inmost thoughts and understanding, He then goes on to say, And their sins and their lawbreaking I will remember no more.

Now where this is absolute remission — forgiveness and cancellation of the penalty — of these [sins and lawbreaking], there is no longer any offering made to atone for sin. Therefore, brethren, since we have full freedom *and* confidence to enter into the [Holy of] Holies [by the power and virtue] in the blood of Jesus, By this fresh (new) and living way which He initiated *and* dedicated and opened for us through the separating curtain (veil of the Holy of Holies), that is, through His flesh, And since we have [such] a great *and* wonderful noble Priest [Who rules] over the house of God.

Let us all come forward *and* draw near with true (honest and sincere) hearts in unqualified assurance *and* absolute conviction engendered by faith [that is, by that leaning of the entire human personality on God in absolute trust and confidence in His power, wisdom, and goodness], having

> our hearts sprinkled *and* purified from a guilty (evil)
> conscience and our bodies cleansed with pure water.
>
> So let us seize *and* hold fast *and* retain without
> wavering the hope we cherish *and* confess *and* our
> acknowledgement of it, for He Who promised is
> reliable (sure) *and* faithful to His word.

In Jeremiah it was promised, and in Hebrews we see exactly how the promise was fulfilled. Jesus made the last blood sacrifice, so we no longer have to give a blood sacrifice. The only sacrifice God requires of us is the sacrifice of our lips giving praise unto Him for that which He has done and accomplished in us and through us. That is the only sacrifice.

> Through Him, therefore, let us constantly and
> at all times offer up to God a sacrifice of praise,
> which is the fruit of lips that thankfully acknow-
> ledge and confess and glorify His name.
>
> Hebrews 13:15 AMP

So Jesus accomplished that final sacrifice within us through His blood so that we can be in a new and living way in Him by the Spirit of God dwelling within us. Everything that we operate in and through in the spirit realm is done by the Holy Spirit. God, the Father wills it, Jesus says it, and then the Holy Spirit brings it forth — causes it to be done in the earth.

Why is that? Because He is our Comforter, our Helper, our Intercessor, our Advocate. Everything that we need on earth, Jesus left with us through the Holy Spirit to accomplish the will of the Father. So if the Father wills it, then the

Holy Spirit can accomplish it through you if you allow Him to do it.

When you receive Jesus into your heart and are born again, three promises are fulfilled in your life: you are cleansed, your spiritual nature is changed, and your sins are forever forgiven. Let's look at how these take place.

CLEANSED BY THE WATER AND THE WORD

ဖ ဖ ဖ

First you are cleansed by the water and the Word. Water is a type of the Word, a type of the Holy Spirit.

> **He saved us, not because of any works of righteousness that we had done, but because of His own pity *and* mercy, by [the] cleansing (bath) of the new birth (regeneration) and renewing of the Holy Spirit.**
>
> **Titus 3:5 AMP**

> **Now ye are clean through the word which I have spoken unto you.**
>
> **John 15:3**

So according to these Scriptures, we are cleansed by the washing and regeneration of the Holy Spirit and by the words Jesus spoke. Well, Jesus and the Word are one, are they not? So through Jesus and the Word you are clean. Hallelujah!

Then Ephesians 5:26 says, **That he might sanctify and cleanse it** [the Church] **with the washing of water by the word.** So Christ cleanses the Church by the washing of the water by the Word. We are the Church individually, and we are the Church collectively.

You are cleansed by the blood of Jesus, but it is by the Word of God that you appropriate this cleansing. When you abide in the Word, then the Word becomes the water by which you, as a believer, are sprinkled and kept clean. It is in this way that we can walk acceptable to God who has mercifully saved us.

So the Word keeps us clean. The reason we don't stay clean is because either we don't stay in the Word or we don't continue to do what the Word says. The Word is pure and holy, and it keeps us pure and holy or clean when we walk in it.

Holiness is not your outward appearance and how you look, but it is what happens on the inside of you. Then because of what has happened on the inside of you, you look different on the outside because there is a shine or a glow of the nature of Jesus coming forth. That is when others will see the beauty of the Lord Jesus Christ shining forth from your countenance and operating through you.

The indwelling of the Spirit is to make us more like God. The only way we can become more like God is through the working of the indwelling Holy Spirit, but often when God begins to work in us, we cry. When a proving time comes, we want to back up and say, "What's happening here?" God is working on the inside of you by the indwelling of the Holy Spirit, causing you to be pure and holy, tried and true.

YOUR SPIRITUAL NATURE IS CHANGED

§ § §

The second promise fulfilled when you are born again is that your spiritual nature is changed because He gives you a new heart or a new spirit. The words "heart" and "spirit" are used interchangeably in the Scriptures. The Word says you have a brand new heart. All things have become new, and old things have passed away as far as your spirit man is concerned.

> **Therefore if any person is (ingrafted) in Christ the Messiah, he is a new creation (a new creature altogether,) the old (previous moral and spiritual condition) has passed away. Behold, the fresh and new has come!**
>
> **2 Corinthians 5:17 AMP**

So now what do you have to do to allow the Holy Spirit to accomplish God's purpose through you? Every day you have to do something about your flesh and your mind because they did not become new when your spirit man did.

Your flesh should not rule you. You have dominion over your flesh, so when your flesh cries out, you can subdue it with the Word of God. Your mind still wants to think the way it used to think and go down the same little trails it used to go down. Get in the Word of God to renew your mind and change those patterns of thinking with the help of the indwelling Holy Spirit. Whether you know it or not, your mind and emotions have a voice too.

One of our biggest problems in the Body of Christ has been that we have operated so much in our emotions, or soulism realm, that when the Spirit moves and the outpouring of the Spirit comes, we do not know the difference. Many times we do not think it is God or the outpouring of the Spirit, because our emotions have not been affected. We think, "Well, it can't be God because I don't feel anything", or "It can't be God because I don't feel like jumping up or shouting hallelujah or singing." It may be that the Spirit of God is moving through a quiet peace doing a deep work, and He wants you to be still. After all, the Holy Spirit doesn't need to jump and shout to do His work in you. Sometimes more is accomplished in a quiet time!

We need to renew our minds by the Word of God and by the Spirit of God so that we can recognize the difference between the Spirit of God moving and our emotions reacting or not reacting. Otherwise, we can get caught in the trap of letting our emotions get so involved when the Spirit moves that we do something within ourselves to keep the move going. When this happens, the Spirit of God is not operating, and the results are of the flesh. We need to yield our spirit to the Holy Spirit within so that we can recognize the flow and move with it.

When you are asked to do something and the Spirit of God is not in it, your spirit will know it, and you will know not to do it. If someone calls you up and asks you to do something and you do not have an unction (anointed leading) by the Spirit of God to do it, then you had better not do it. Do not try to work up something or speak out of your own human spirit.

One of the most frequently asked questions I get from people is this: "How can I know I am being led by the Holy Spirit and not just reacting to my own flesh or being deceived by Satan?" My answer is always, "Go to the Word."

Beloved, do not put faith in every spirit, but prove (test) the spirits to discover whether they proceed from God; for many false prophets have

gone forth into the world. By this you may know (perceive and recognize) the Spirit of God: every spirit which acknowledges *and* confesses [the fact] that Jesus Christ, the Messiah, [actually] has become man *and* has come in the flesh is of God — has God for its source. And every spirit which does not acknowledge *and* confess *that* Jesus *Christ has come in the flesh* [but would annul, destroy, sever, disunite Him] is not of God — does not proceed from Him. This [non-confession] is the [spirit] of the antichrist, [of] which you heard that it was coming, and now it is already in the world.

Little children, you are of God — you belong to Him — and have [already] defeated *and* overcome them [the agents of the antichrist], because He Who lives in you is greater (mightier) than he who is in the world. They proceed from the world *and* are of the world, therefore it is out of the world [its whole economy morally considered] that they speak, and the world listens (pays attention) to them.

We are [children] of God. Whoever is learning to know God — progressively to perceive, recognize, and understand God by observation and experience — and to get an ever clearer knowledge of Him — listens to us; and he who is not of God does not listen *or* pay attention to us. By this we know (recognize) the Spirit of Truth and the spirit of error.

1 John 4:1-6 AMP

We all have a responsibility to test the spirits. If you ever have a question of whose voice you are hearing, simply ask it to acknowledge and confess that Jesus Christ has come in the flesh. If you don't get any acknowledgment, you will know it is not the voice or prompting of the Holy Spirit. Also, if anything you are feeling prompted to do or being asked by someone else to do does not line up with the Word or goes against the nature and character of God, don't do it. The Holy Spirit is the Truth and will never lead you to do something that contradicts the Word.

> **This is He Who came by (with) water and blood [His baptism and His death], Jesus Christ, the Messiah; not by (in) the water only, but by (in) the water and the blood. And it is the [Holy] Spirit Who bears witness, because the [Holy] Spirit is the Truth.**
>
> **1 John 5:6 AMP**

YOUR SINS ARE REMITTED

§ § §

The third promise fulfilled when we are born again is that your sins are forgiven. We know that God's Word is true, and He is faithful to perform that Word in you, so when you ask for your sins to be forgiven, they are forgiven.

> **...Receive (admit) the Holy Spirit! [Now, having received the Holy Spirit and being led and directed by Him] if you forgive the sins of any one they are forgiven; if you retain the sins of any one, they are retained.**
>
> **John 20:22-23 AMP**

Notice that in connection with the forgiveness of sins, you are to receive the Holy Spirit. We have to establish that the Holy Spirit is indwelling you the minute that Christ comes into your life and that the Holy Spirit is there for a purpose. He needs to operate and work within you. But when the fullness comes, then the outpouring can begin to be effectual within you by the Spirit of God.

When someone is born again, his sins are forgiven. But if he does not believe, then he is not born again, and his sins are retained. We need to tell people that if they do not receive Christ, they will just go on living in sin. We need to tell them that Jesus died on the cross and shed His blood for them so that they could have forgiveness of sin, but they have to receive the Lord Jesus Christ so those sins can be forgiven. Otherwise, they will retain their sins because they cannot get rid of them within themselves.

We are righteous because of Jesus, not because of anything within ourselves. Being born again is a heart experience and not done by head knowledge alone. I have seen people just pray the salvation prayer at meetings because they think it is the right thing to do at the time or because everybody else is doing it. This is like a teenager who says, "Well, why can't I do it? Everybody's doing it. It's the thing to do." But just saying with their mouth, "I receive Jesus," is not going to do it. They must make a heart decision and then there must be fruit demonstrated in their lives to prove they really did accept Jesus into their hearts. Otherwise, their sins are retained.

People have said to me, "Well, I thought I was born again. I went down front and shook the pastor's hand and said the prayer." The critical difference is whether they made that heart decision which allows Jesus and the indwelling presence of the Holy Spirit to change them from being confused and hesitant to being filled with joy. Lives are changed only when hearts are changed.

Giving people the direct truth brings understanding. We need to carefully explain what we mean by being born again or by being saved. These are Bible terms, and we have to remember that we are speaking to an unregenerate world. They do not know these terms because most of them do not know what the Word of God says. Many do not even know Who Jesus is. They think He was just a man who walked in Bible days on the earth, like any other prophet. It is important that we bring the right understanding to people. It is the knowledge of the Word that will cause unbelievers to receive the Lord by the Holy Spirit. Speaking the Word affects that desire within them to accept Jesus because they have a clear understanding.

All believers need to understand what Jesus did for us so that the Holy Spirit can fully operate in their lives. Where there is remission of sin, there is no more offering for sin because Jesus was the final sacrifice for sin. Therefore, there are no more sacrifices for sin to be made.

All we have to do is receive the Lord Jesus Christ, acknowledge that He is the Son of God, and receive Him as our Savior. We must turn ourselves around and go the opposite direction from that sin we were living in and let the new heart that He has given to us begin to rule and reign in our lives. This is what Jesus did for us, and this is what brings the Spirit within us, causing us to experience all of His benefits in this life.

LOOK FOR THE SUPERNATURAL, NOT THE SPECTACULAR

໑ ໑ ໑

It is so important to establish and understand the indwelling of the Spirit of God. We get too carried away looking for the spectacular move of God when we have not even established what we are supposed to be doing with the indwelling. We should be looking for the supernatural instead of the spectacular.

There is so much sin and carnality in the Body of Christ because many of us have not allowed the Holy Spirit to do what He was sent to do within us. And we will not see the fullness of the outpouring until we understand what He was sent to do within us.

When you are developing the fullness of the Holy Spirit inside you, He will cause those spectacular things to come to pass as He wills. But they will not operate through you until you let the indwelling of the Spirit that came into your life when you were born again do His work in you. Then you will be transformed, and you will have everything that God intended for you to have in this life as an overcomer. You will operate in the fullness of the Holy Spirit, and the outpouring will always be there reaching out.

Growing God's Way

๖ ๖ ๖

From birth to death, life is a growing process —physically, emotionally, intellectually and spiritually. Throughout every step of that process, many diverse choices are set before us. When a baby first stands alone teetering on tiny feet with a look of wonder in his eyes, suddenly he has a new set of choices to make — whether to bravely attempt his first steps toward independence or whether to sit back down and continue crawling to get where he wants to go.

The first choice is fearfully new and may even be painful as knees get scraped and heads get bumped. The second choice is easier, a little more comfortable, definitely safer, and it obviously works, but it lacks the challenge and excitement of reaching new levels of growth and maturity. The more determined and adventuresome baby will take the risk and step out. The more timid and fearful baby will sit back down and wait for another day.

As Christians we have similar, continuing choices to make in our spiritual growing process. When we accept Jesus as our Savior, we receive the indwelling of the Holy Spirit. At that point, we have just pulled ourselves up onto our spiritual feet, and the Holy Spirit is saying, "Come on, just take one little step. I'm right here to catch you. Come to me. I have so much more for you to experience." It is our choice whether to step out and experience a new level of growth or to stay safely on our knees crawling with the other baby Christians.

SPIRITUAL BABY SHOES

ᔑ ᔑ ᔑ

Perhaps right now you are standing there teetering in your spiritual baby shoes saying, "Oh, do I dare step into the water and get into all that 'tongue talking' business?" Or perhaps you have already taken that first step and received the "infilling" of the Holy Spirit and now are saying, "Okay, God, now what do I do?" You can choose to remain in your baby shoes or allow the Holy Spirit to give you a new heart and a new spirit with the power to fulfill His purposes through you — bringing others into the kingdom.

FROM SOULISH TO SELFLESS

ᔑ ᔑ ᔑ

Are you willing to let the Holy Spirit change your soulish nature so you will become as selfless as God is and as Jesus was on the earth? Two of the major problems in the Body of Christ are that we have been thinking too much about ourselves and operating too much in the fear of man. That is why we have not stood up and been bold enough to speak the truth. We are too caught up in thinking, "What will they say?" Or, "What will they think of me?" But if you know your Father God, you know that He will protect you and won't let you go through anything which you can't handle or with which you can't cope. If you are constantly saying, "I can't," to God, what you are really saying is that Jesus and the Word are of no effect in your life.

RECOGNIZE THE DAY!

֍ ֍ ֍

It is time to wake up and recognize the day in which we are living. We are living in the end times, and the Bible clearly says we must be on guard lest we be deceived and led astray.

> **Jesus answered them, Be careful that no one misleads you — deceiving you and leading you into error. For many will come in (on the strength of) My name — appropriating the name which belongs to Me — saying, I am the Messiah, the Christ; and they will lead many astray.**
>
> **And then many will be offended *and* repelled *and* begin to distrust *and* desert [Him Whom they ought to trust and obey] *and* will stumble and fall away, and betray one another *and* pursue one another with hatred. And many false prophets will rise up and deceive *and* lead many into error.**
>
> **For false Christs and false prophets will arise, and they will show great signs and wonders, so as to deceive *and* lead astray, if possible, even the elect (God's chosen ones).**
>
> **Matthew 24:4-5,10-11,24 AMP**

Paul gave a similar warning to the early Christians.

Indeed all who delight in piety *and* are determined to live a devoted *and* godly life in Christ Jesus will meet with persecution — will be made to suffer because of their religious stand. But wicked men and imposters will go on from bad to worse, deceiving *and* leading astray others and being deceived *and* led astray themselves. But as for you, continue to hold to the things that you have learned and of which you are convinced, knowing from whom you learned [them].

2 Timothy 3:12-14 AMP

Why will we be deceived? Because we only know *about* God. We don't *know* Him. You get to *know* Him through the indwelling presence of the Holy Spirit, as the nine fruits of the Spirit begin to be brought into maturity in your life. You can't do it within yourself. It is done by the Spirit as you allow His presence to work in you. This is clearly stated in Galatians 5:22-26 AMP.

But the fruit of the (Holy) Spirit, [the work which His presence within accomplishes] — is love, joy (gladness), peace, patience (an even temper, forbearance), kindness, goodness (benevolence), faithfulness; (Meekness, humility), gentleness, self-control (self-restraint, continence). Against such things there is no law [that can bring a charge].

And those who belong to Christ Jesus, the Messiah, have crucified the flesh — the godless human nature — with its passions and appetites and desires. If we live by the (Holy) Spirit, let us also walk by the Spirit. — If by the Holy Spirit we have our life [in God], let us go forward walking in line,

our conduct controlled by the Spirit. Let us not
become vainglorious and self-conceited, competitive
and challenging *and* provoking *and* irritating to one
another, envying *and* being jealous of one another.

UNITY NOT COMPETITION

ᛒ   ᛒ   ᛒ

I want to make an important point here. God doesn't
want us to put tags on other people because we are all in the
Body of Christ. It is because of such tags — charismatics,
Word of faith people, evangelicals, Holy Rollers, Baptists,
Methodists, Catholics, etc. — that there is so much separa-
tion. One of these days, we are going to learn that we are all
one family, one Body in one kingdom — the kingdom of
God. What we need is unity not competition.

We all have the same Holy Spirit, and there is only ONE.
We have all been given the same Commission. Jesus didn't
say anything about how many or how well we do it or that
we are to be concerned about how the other guy is doing it.
It is *doing* it that is important. The spirit of competition
comes from the world, and it causes separation, jealousy
and envy.

SHORT-CIRCUITED POWER

ᛒ   ᛒ   ᛒ

Do you know that one of the reasons why the power of
God in the believer hasn't been as effective as it should be is
because we have not matured in the inward man? Our
power has been short-circuited. It doesn't have any punch

to it because the full power of the Holy Spirit cannot work in impurity. It is thwarted because we haven't allowed the indwelling presence to mature us, to bring us into right living with God on a daily basis, and to operate in the fullness of His presence so we are keen to Him. We haven't put our total trust in God. There are still things we are questioning or trying to do within ourselves. God has called us to live and walk by the Holy Spirit. When we are fully controlled by the Holy Spirit, then our full trust will be in the Father God.

One reason we don't get to that point is because we are so concerned with how we will look, and here is the big one — whether someone will think we are "weird!" But you need to recognize that those who are weird are "trying" to show by their weirdness that they are spiritual. When you have a relationship with God through the indwelling presence of the Holy Spirit, you are who you are IN GOD, and you are spiritual. You don't have to "try" to be spiritual by doing weird things. You are just who you are IN GOD, and you just do it.

SPIRITUALITY MEASURED BY MATURITY

๑ ๑ ๑

What proves you are spiritual is how you handle things. Your spirituality is measured by your maturity. It is not because you are used in the gifts of the Spirit or because you have such a great oracle of teaching or because miracles happen, but because you *know* God.

I've seen baby Christians yield to the Holy Spirit and be used in the gifts. Sometimes they didn't even know what was going on or what was happening to them. And unfortunately sometimes because they were not in a church where they got good teaching on the Holy Spirit, they did become weird because they began to listen to other spirits. You must have a strong foundation from the Word of what the Holy Spirit is all about.

And then some of us show our immaturity by talking about those who have strayed instead of going to them and trying to restore them with the knowledge of the Word of God. There are people that need to be restored in the Body from being hurt, from getting weird because they didn't know any better. Everybody talks about them or laughs at them or turns their backs on them. They don't know what to do. They are helpless.

We forget we are all family. If it was in the natural, you would put your arm around this person and say, "I'm not going to let people talk about you like that. I know you, and I know that it is not your heart to be like this. I want to help you." We must allow the indwelling presence of the Holy Spirit to mature us to the point where we can go to that person and say, "Look, I want to speak truth to you in love. This is the truth. You need a foundation here. You are struggling, and you don't know what to do about it. There may be some things happening in your life that aren't of God. Let me help you." Then you begin to share with them the truth of the Word of God.

You need to be a doer of the Word so you will grow and mature in all things. Sure you may stub your toe here and there. You may miss it and get into the flesh occasionally. But the Holy Spirit is with you to guide you into truth, and

He will help you if you ask Him to and if you will stay in His presence.

There are three things that we need to do when we talk about the Spirit within so we can keep ourselves strong and operating in His indwelling presence. First, we need to have a constant renewal of the Holy Spirit. Second, we need to learn to walk in the Spirit so that we can be fully informed of the manner in which God would have us to live. Third, we need to learn the way of the Spirit so that we can trace God in all circumstances which form our daily walk with Him. If we are going to appropriate the benefits of the Holy Spirit in our lives, we need to do these three things daily.

CHAPTER 4

Renewed Every Morning

§ § §

In order to benefit from the Holy Spirit's coming to indwell us at the New Birth, there must be a daily renewing through studying God's Word, which quickens us, and through seeking God in prayer. So another word that we could use for being renewed would be quickening, quickened by the Word of God and quickened by the Spirit of God. We have to obtain or diligently seek renewal by the Holy Spirit on a continual basis.

We do not receive the fullness of the Holy Spirit at the New Birth. The verse below refers to salvation and says "renewing" of the Holy Spirit, not "receiving" of the Holy Spirit.

> **He saved us, not because of any works of right-eousness that we had done, but because of His own pity and mercy, by [the] cleansing (bath) of the new birth (regeneration) and renewing of the Holy Spirit.**
>
> **Titus 3:5 AMP**

SEALED WITH HIS PROMISE

§ § §

After salvation, we are sealed with the Holy Spirit of promise. So the Holy Spirit is there, and He can bring you into that quickening, that renewal. Ephesians 1:13 states:

> In whom ye also trusted, after that ye heard
> the word of truth, the gospel of your salvation: in
> whom also after that ye believed, ye were sealed
> with that Holy Spirit of promise.

Ephesians 5:18 says that we should be filled with the Spirit.

> **And be not drunk with wine, wherein is excess;
> but be filled with the Spirit.**

The Greek language has many tenses. Like the English language, it has past, present and future as well as a continuing tense. When you look at the word, "filled," in the Greek, it means "continually" filled. The verse should read like this, "You should be not drunk with wine wherein is excess but be constantly in the process of being filled with the Spirit or full of the Spirit."

CONTINUALLY FILLED

Ephesians 5:19-20 tells us how to do this:

> **Speaking to yourselves in psalms and hymns
> and spiritual songs, singing and making melody in
> your heart to the Lord; Giving thanks always for
> all things unto God and the Father in the name of
> our Lord Jesus Christ.**

You can do that by praying in tongues, by building yourself up, keeping yourself aware of the Holy Spirit, knowing you are full of the Holy Spirit. With the filling of the Spirit, comes the anointing. Because of the quickening in your mind and your body, you can worship the Father.

You can renew your relationship with Him every day by taking the time to yield yourself to Him, to pray, sing and rejoice in the Spirit. In this way, you will not only be renewed in your spirit, but you will maintain your joy as well. Nehemiah 8:10 says **the joy of the Lord is your strength**. A spirit of praise and joy renews, quickens and strengthens the believer.

THE INNER AND OUTER MAN QUICKENED

ら ら ら

The inner man and outer man are quickened by the indwelling of God's Spirit. Romans 8:11 says:

> **But if the Spirit of him that raised up Jesus from the dead dwell in you, he that raised up Christ from the dead shall also quicken your mortal bodies by his Spirit that dwelleth in you.**

That means our outer man (mortal body) is quickened by the Holy Spirit also.

Second Corinthians 4:16 states:

> **For which cause we faint not; but though our outward man perish, yet the inward man is renewed day by day.**

Ephesians 3:14-16 states:

> **For this cause I bow my knees unto the Father of our Lord Jesus Christ, Of whom the whole family in heaven and earth is named, That he would grant you, according to the riches of his**

glory, to be strengthened with might by his Spirit
in the inner man.

The two verses above show us that the inner man is
renewed day by day and strengthened with might by the
working of the Holy Spirit.

You have to realize that we are not named just in
heaven, but we are named also in the earth. If you are
operating in the fullness of the Word of God, the Devil
knows you. He knows who you are. The only reason the
Devil doesn't know who you are is because you are not
operating in the fullness of the Word and taking your
dominion in this earth.

When your name has an "and in the earth" attached to
it, God grants you according to the riches of His glory to be
strengthened with might by His Spirit in the inner man. In
that renewing comes might. We are strengthened by the
might of His Spirit.

SOARING LIKE THE EAGLES

၍ ၍ ၍

Now let's look at Isaiah 40:28-31 AMP:

> Have you not known? Have you not heard?
> The everlasting God, the Lord, the Creator of the
> ends of the earth, does not faint or grow weary;
> there is no searching of His understanding. He
> gives power to the faint *and* weary, and to him who
> has no might He increases strength — causing it to
> multiply and making it to abound.

Even youths shall faint and be weary, and *selected* young men shall feebly stumble *and* fall exhausted; But those who wait for the Lord — who expect, look for, and hope in Him shall change and renew their strength *and* power; they shall lift their wings *and* mount up [close to God] as eagles [mount up to the sun]; they shall run *and* not be weary, they shall walk and not faint *or* become tired.

Through the renewing of the Holy Spirit when we are weak or weary, we are given power and might if we yield ourselves to the Spirit. Not only will He give us the power and might we need, but He multiplies it and makes it abound. Hallelujah! Our God is a mighty God, and He never grows faint or weary!

Verses 30-31 say that the young men will exchange their weakness and faintness and weariness for the power of God, for the might and strength that only comes through the Spirit of God. We can exchange our weakness and weariness, but we must look for and expect it and hope in God. Knowing that there is hope through His Word and by His Spirit, you will find it and exchange it for all the strength, might and power you need.

Then it says, **they shall lift their wings and mount up [close to God] as eagles [mount up to the sun.]** The sun represents light that renews and brings power. **They shall run and not be weary, they shall walk and not faint or become tired.** There is that multiplication and abounding. Glory to God!

We should not grow weary in well doing. If we are constantly exchanging our weakness, our faintness and our weariness for the power, might and strength of the Father God by the Holy Spirit, God says He will multiply His power, might and strength in us and cause us to abound in it. Now that is something to get excited about!

Did you know that eagles never fly against the current? But how often do we do just that by trying to do things in our own might or our own way? The eagle flows with the current because he knows that the current is not going to stay where it is. It is going to go a little higher, and it will pull him up higher. When we learn to flow with the current of the Holy Spirit, we won't stay where we are because the Holy Spirit doesn't stay at one level. He will bring us up closer to God, closer to that light.

RENEWED LIKE THE EAGLE

ভ ভ ভ

The eagle also renews himself by shaking himself to shake off all the things that attach themselves to his wings and feathers. He shakes himself all over until everything falls off. As we begin to shake ourselves in the might of the Holy Spirit and the Word of God, all the weights that have attached themselves to us will begin to fall off. Then we can soar in that flow of the Holy Spirit. The eagle renews himself every day, and we need to do the same thing. We need to recognize how important it is to be renewed in the Spirit daily so that we can multiply and abound in His might and strength and flow with Him.

I get excited when I read this Scripture because I can see myself through the Word and by prayer, shaking myself and getting rid of those things that attach themselves to me that are weights causing me not to be able to hear and flow with the Spirit. Then I see myself not going against the circumstance, but just flowing with the Spirit in that circumstance. As I learn to flow with the Spirit in that circumstance, in the might and power of the Holy Spirit, of the Father God, and of the Word of God; then I soar in that circumstance. As I allow the Holy Spirit to flow in my life, He brings me above the circumstance, closer to God, where I can see clearly what I am supposed to do rather than succumb to the circumstance.

FINDING THE RIGHT BALANCE

୬ ୬ ୬

This is how we can be victorious by renewing ourselves every day in the Word and soaring with the Holy Spirit, getting closer to God the Father. We can't have one without the other — the Word of God and the Holy Spirit — they go together. There are some people who say, "It's the Word, the Word, the Word." Bless God I am a Word person, but without the Holy Spirit, it becomes legalistic bondage with no life in it. Then, on the other hand, there are people who only know the Spirit of God and say, "We just let the Holy Spirit flow, whatever..." And then there is no order and no foundation. God is a God of order, and He expects us to have a foundation in His Word. We need the Holy Spirit to bring the Word to life in us.

We now see clearly that the inner man and the outer man are quickened by the indwelling presence of the Holy Spirit and that there is a dual purpose of the workings of the Holy Spirit — the working of the indwelling presence for the benefit of the individual believer and the workings of the outpouring of the Holy Spirit with power from on high to bless others. We must do something every day to keep ourselves aware that is what needs to be happening in our lives.

HE IS OUR RIGHTEOUSNESS

A daily renewal of the Holy Spirit will bring us awareness of the fullness of God and awareness that we are righteous. It will bring us awareness that Jesus lives on the inside of us and that we are one with Him because He has made us that way. He is our righteousness; we are righteous because of Him, not because of anything we have done. It is His righteousness that causes us to go forth and be what we need to be. We can do whatever is needed because we have the Spirit in us just as it says in Philippians 4:13:

I can do all things through Christ which strengtheneth me.

The Holy Spirit is there waiting for us to draw on Him because He is our helper. But He can't help us if we don't ask and then give Him instructions. In the natural, it would be like saying to someone who works for you, "I want you to help me," but he just stands there. You are thinking, "Well, why isn't he helping me. I brought him over here to help me?" It is because you haven't given him any instructions. He doesn't know what you want him to do. The Holy Spirit is on the inside of you to be your helper, but you have to ask and then give Him instructions.

Just because the Holy Spirit is on the inside of you doesn't mean that you are just going to be mature overnight in the family of God. In the natural, a baby can't do the same things a fourteen year old can do. It is the same way spiritually. There is a growing process which can be sped up when we allow the Holy Spirit to work in us, to bring forth knowledge instead of trying to do it within ourselves.

So, begin to pray in the Spirit, begin to sing in the Spirit, begin to quicken yourself, begin to speak your joy and your gratification unto the Lord, and praise Him for who He is and not for what He has done. As you do this, there will be a quickening that will come within you, and you will begin to see and be aware that the Holy Spirit is there.

EXERCISE YOURSELF IN THE SPIRIT

§ § §

I find that when I pray in the Spirit, He quickens me. Then I go to the Word of God and start reading it, so my mind stays renewed and I am edified by it. When you exercise yourself in the Spirit, He brings life into you. When you exercise the Holy Spirit within your life, you can't stay down, and you can't stay depressed. You will be full of joy, you will operate in it, and everything you are looking at in the Word will be exciting to you.

I just get excited talking about it because I know Him, and I know Who He is, and I know what He has done for me. I'm not as mature as I need to be or as I want to be, but I have learned to allow the Holy Spirit to be to me what I need at that time — whether that is comfort, quickening, renewing, helping me pray, whatever — He is there.

I am an inspirational teacher in the gifts, and sometimes when we are in seminars, I am given a subject to teach and I think, "Oh, God. I can't do this!" But then the Holy Spirit says, "Wait a minute. You can do this." Anyone who knows me or has heard me teach knows that no matter what subject I start with, I'm going to come back around to the love of God or to the Holy Spirit. After all, everything in the Word involves the Holy Spirit and the love of God, because God is love and the Holy Spirit is the one that causes things to be done on the earth according to the will of the Father. So the Holy Spirit always reminds me of the truth, and I am able to do it because the Holy Spirit causes me to be able. He is my Helper.

We have the indwelling presence of the Holy Spirit after our new birth. Then we are indued with power after being filled with the Holy Spirit. The only prerequisite for being filled with the Holy Spirit is being born again. The Holy Spirit is a gift to the believer, and as we exercise that gift and continually get renewed, He will cause us to maintain our joy. If you ever feel like you are weak in faith, check up on your joy because if you are weak in joy, then you have no strength to operate your faith.

GOD'S NATURE IN US

§ § §

By the indwelling of the Holy Spirit, we have the nine fruits of the Spirit, the nature of God, on the inside of us. The fruits can be perfected in our lives so that we can walk in these characteristics of the nature of God. We must let the Holy Spirit do His work in us and mature us or perfect us.

The nine manifestations of the Spirit bring forth signs and wonders in your life that will bless others as we read in Mark 16.

> **And these signs shall follow them that believe....And they went forth, and preached everywhere, the Lord working with them, and confirming the word with signs following. Amen.**
>
> **Mark 16:17,20**

It does not say in the Word that we are to be seeking signs and wonders, it says that signs and wonders are to follow those who believe. Many of us have gotten it backwards. That is the reason we get all caught up in things and are deceived. We follow after things that aren't really of God because we are looking for signs and wonders. We don't need signs and wonders when we have the Word of God and the Holy Spirit on the inside of us.

The key to being victorious in any situation is to remain full of the Spirit. That is why Ephesians tells us to be in the process of being filled with the Holy Spirit all the time. And if we are going to maintain the joy that comes through the fullness of the Holy Spirit, then we have to continually praise the Lord. There should be within us a spirit of praise to the Father God and joy all the time.

IN THE FAMILY OF GOD

§ § §

When we are in the family of God, God is involved with us every day. If we understand how the Spirit of God works in us, then we are aware when God is working in us. As we pray in the Spirit and read the Word each day and follow through on what the Spirit reveals to us, then we can run the race to the full measure.

Everyday when I wake up, before I even get out of bed, the first thing on my lips is, "Thank you, Father God, for this day. Because You have blessed me, this is a blessed day. Thank you, Father God, because You saw fit to give unto me all the wonderful things that I have and enjoy because You love me. Not because of what I have done that's right, not because I am so pure and holy, not because I am perfect, but because You love me."

That is the Father God, and we need to be aware of Him because in that awareness we can begin to allow the Holy Spirit to work in us so that we begin to know fully the heart of God. Then we can have a relationship with Him because we know Him, and we know His voice. We don't waste time because we have taken the time each day to love and appreciate Him and to be grateful for that with which He has blessed us, not because we have earned it but because of His mercy and grace.

NEW EVERY MORNING

᷉ ᷉ ᷉

A familiar Scripture in Lamentations tells us that the Lord's mercies are new every morning. We need to thank Him every morning and continually be renewed with hope in Him.

It is because of the Lord's mercy and loving-kindness that we are not consumed, because His

> [tender] compassions fail not. They are new every
> morning; great and abundant is Your stability and
> faithfulness. The Lord is my portion or share, says
> my living being (my inner self); therefore will I
> hope in Him and wait expectantly for Him.
>
> Lamentations 3:22-24 AMP

So every morning as you begin to pray in the Spirit and praise Him, the joy of the Lord fills your life and your soul. Then you get up and begin to read the Word of God, and it is beautiful.

Many times, in those morning times, the Holy Spirit begins to speak to me about what I am to do that day. It is often very different from what I would have planned to do, and it may not be what I want to do that day, but I am learning the way of the Spirit in my life and in my daily walk with Him so I can live as He would have me to live on this earth.

QUALITY NOT QUANTITY

Our inner man is renewed every day by the Word of God and by prayer, and it is the quality of our time with Him not just the quantity. Quality time involves getting your mind quiet and totally concentrating on just you and the Holy Spirit, just you and the Word of God with no distractions.

How many times have you sat down to read the Word but your mind keeps distracting you? When you can't keep your mind in line, get up and rejoice. Begin to pray in the Spirit and sing in the Spirit. Why do we emphasize singing in the Spirit? Because it ministers to your spirit man *and* to your soul.

It is by that daily renewal with Him, continually worshipping and being aware of Him and being full of Him, that we know Him. The Holy Spirit indwelling within us is what enables us to have a relationship with the Lord Jesus Christ and with the Father God. By that every day quickening and renewal, we know we are on the right track. We walk forth energized with His power, with His might and with His goodness.

CHAPTER 5

Walk in the Spirit

ဤ ဤ ဤ

To obtain the benefits of the Holy Spirit's indwelling presence, we must learn to walk in the Spirit, which means to live according to God's plan of salvation. A lot of people think being born again is all there is to salvation, but it is only the beginning of God's plan of salvation. When we are born again, we are restored back into His family, back into His likeness through Christ Jesus. When we walk according to God's plan of salvation, God will speak to our heart by His Spirit and keep us in His perfect will in all things.

We must learn to walk in the Spirit so we can be fully informed of the manner in which God would have us to live. Many of us think that just because we are born again and Spirit filled, we know how to live. We do not if we are not letting the Holy Spirit work in us. If we are not building ourselves up, the next thing we know, our emotions or our bodies will take hold of us and rule us. That is not the manner in which God intends for us to live.

Walking in the Spirit is not being on some kind of a cloud and just floating along. That is carnality in people who want other people to think they are spiritual. When you learn to walk in the Spirit, you are what you are. You are a spirit being operating in the "real" you who is the spirit man on the inside of you. Walking in the Spirit just works in you. It is not any type of appearance. Remember the unbeliever will be drawn to you because of the joy that you have.

BE REAL

§ § §

God is a real God, and He is a Spirit, and because we are spirits made in his image, we have to be real.

We have to know that we have the Father God and the Lord Jesus Christ dwelling on the inside of us and that the indwelling of the Holy Spirit is for our benefit. But do we know what those benefits are, and are we letting them work in us to effect in us that which God desired us to have when He sent His Son?

These benefits are not just so you can turn away from sin and say, "I've turned from sin." No, there are things we have to establish and let be effectual in our lives before we will experience the fullness of the outpouring.

We have to get rid of this thinking that we already know it all. No matter what you tell some people about what the Spirit of the Lord is saying or has done, they always say, "I know that." But this can't always be true because God has not revealed everything to everybody.

We act like this because of pride. We do not want others to know that we might not have known that the Spirit moved a certain way, or we might not have recognized how the

Spirit moved right then. That is selfish pride, and it is carnal. We have to be real and honest with ourselves and God.

THE VALUE OF GODLINESS

ы ы ы

For physical training is of some value — useful for a little; but godliness [spiritual training] is useful *and* of value in everything *and* in every way, for it holds promise for the present life and also for the life which is to come.

1 Timothy 4:8 AMP

Why is godliness or spiritual training of more value? Because you are trained by the Spirit in how you should live on this earth. Otherwise, you rely on the flesh, which is your carnal man without the nature of God. The problem that we have in this day in which we are living is that too many saints of God have placed the bodily exercise of their physical man on the same level as their spirit man. They are not on the same level, because what you are saying is, "My physical man is more important, and I will be ruled by my physical man instead of my spirit man."

And that is what has happened in the Church today. We have allowed the thinking of the world to come into our thinking in the Church, and we have the idea that if we are not a certain way or don't look a certain way, then we are not fit for the kingdom.

I have heard preachers get up and say, "Well, if you don't weigh a hundred and eighty pounds then you're not fit to be in the pulpit." Well, who said so? But see, they have allowed the thinking of the world to come in on them, and they are more taken up with how they look in their physical man than how pleasing they are to God in their spirit man.

That is not godliness. And the world has put such pressure on the human race to exercise that people have fallen so in love with their bodies that they cannot see or hear anything else. They are deceived into thinking they are doing it to be pleasing to God by presenting their body as a living sacrifice unto God. But they get so caught up with training the physical body that they forget about the spiritual training of their spirit man which is more important.

If you allow the indwelling presence of the Holy Spirit to mature you and work in you and in your soulish realm, then you can do something with your physical body. The problem is we will discipline ourselves to the Word of God and prayer, but we won't discipline ourselves in saying, "Well, I can eat in moderation." Or we will not discipline ourselves to lead a fasted life. We say, "I need to fast and pray to quit being so conscious of my body and to get in the Word of God." But there is still an ulterior motive of thinking, "This will help me lose weight." So we go on a three-day fast, but when we come off of that fast, we eat like there is no tomorrow. We don't continue to live a fasted life.

A lot of people who have a problem with gaining weight look at a thin person and think, "Oh, you've got it made." Do you know there are a lot of thin people who are gluttons? And just because someone is overweight does not mean he or she is a glutton. It doesn't matter whether you are overweight or thin, what matters is whether you are allowing the Spirit of God to work in you so that you are disciplined in every area of your life. God gave us a free will, so we have to make the decision that we will be diligent to discipline ourselves to allow the Holy Spirit to do His work in us.

A God of Variety

⑨ ⑨ ⑨

God is a God of variety. He did not create us to all look alike. Isn't that wonderful? He didn't make us to all act alike or sound alike. Wouldn't that be boring? So how can I say to you, "You are not where you need to be because you're ten pounds overweight." Whether or not I weigh 10 pounds more than what some chart says I should is not what is vital. What is vital is the life of God flowing in me and the godliness of the Father God working in me.

When you are caught up with the spirit man, you are caught up with God, and when you learn to renew yourself every day by the Word and by the Spirit of God, you can operate in the joy and fullness of His Spirit, and your soul is satisfied. You begin to sing in the Spirit, and as you grow in that, then you begin to interpret that song. Then pretty soon you have grown enough so that you don't even have to pray in the Spirit and interpret it; it just comes out by simple prophecy. You are rejoicing by the Spirit of God, and that satisfies the soul. You are fulfilled. When the Bible says that you can be totally fulfilled in Christ Jesus, it means just that.

By allowing worldly thoughts to come into the Church, we have gotten our eyes off of the spirit man and are not allowing the Spirit of God to work in us. We act just like the world, measuring everybody by how they look and whether they are fit or not. How you look is not what makes you fit for the kingdom of God. It is whether or not you are allowing the Word of God and the Holy Spirit to be effective within you. *That* is what is important. *That* is what causes you to be what you need to be in the kingdom of God.

Now because you have the Spirit of God and because you want to be your best, you will do everything you know to do to look your best. God gave us common sense. We need to discipline ourselves in all things. He wants us to be clean and healthy, to have good personal habits and to take care of ourselves.

We are not to measure ourselves or others by the standards of the world. Too often we put everything in one pile and measure it the same way. Let's use prayer as an example. If we tried to use the same prayer to fit every situation, we wouldn't be very effective, because there are different prayers needed for different situations. When we haven't allowed ourselves to learn to walk in the Spirit, to be informed of how God would have us live on this earth, carrying out the full plan of His salvation in our lives, we tend to be influenced by the things of this world and that is carnality in its purest form.

The real issue is that you are not to put *anything* on the same level as your spiritual life in Christ Jesus. You must allow the Spirit of God to work in you so that you live according to God's plan of salvation every day of your life.

DON'T PREACH CONVICTIONS

๑ ๑ ๑

The reason we are not supposed to preach our convictions is because people have different convictions, and what I am convicted of may be different than what you are convicted of. Everybody is unique, and it is a personal relationship with God according to that individual — according to how mature he is, according to his personality, according to how he has been brought up in his family, and according to his culture. So you can't just put everyone in a box and begin to say, "This is how God deals with me, so this is the way it must be for you too." That is not right. This is how God deals with me because this is the way I am. He deals with me the way He does because of my personality and how I think and how I respond to things. And however He works with you, that is the reason He works with you in that way. So we need to understand these things and not come into bondage to them.

When you come into bondage, it amplifies, whether it is being overweight or not educated enough or not financially secure. You can't get your mind off of it. You *think* about it all the time, but You don't *do* anything about it. It just gets worse because you have allowed the distraction to monopolize your mind, then it begins to affect your body or other areas of your life.

What you have to do is pick yourself up and allow the indwelling presence of the Holy Spirit within you to begin to work in you to renew you. That renewing quickens your body so that you can effectively make changes in the areas needed. God expects us to do that as individuals.

WORK OUT YOUR OWN SALVATION

§ § §

Why does Philippians 2:12 say, **Work out your own salvation with fear and trembling?** Because it is a personal relationship, and you have to work that out according to what you see in the Word, according to your maturity, according to where you are and according to the knowledge that you have. But it is all done by the Spirit of God, according to Philippians 2:13 AMP:

> [Not in your own strength] for it is God Who is all the while effectually at work in you [energizing and creating in you the power and desire], both to will and to work for His good pleasure and satisfaction and delight.

If you are a minister of the gospel, whatever God has called you to do is important, but if you are in a rut and think, "Well, this is what I have to do, and I can't do anything else," then you are not walking in the Spirit, and you are not letting the Spirit of God do a work in you. No matter who you are or what you are doing, you need to be refreshed every day because God's mercies are new every morning. Through the Spirit of God, He gives us freshness every day. We need to walk with the things of God in that freshness.

Some teachers have gotten so caught up in rituals, they think everything has to be written out in a certain way, and they miss the Spirit. They may have a wonderful sermon, yet the Spirit of God may be leading them in a different flow so that they can meet the needs of the people in that service at that moment. But they just carry on with their sermon when the Spirit of God wanted to change the flow. I often wonder if they even prayed about how God would have them do it.

We are living in a day when, if you do not learn to walk in the Spirit and you do not have an intimate relationship with the Lord Jesus Christ, then you will be left standing on the bank of the river. We have small thinking compared to God, but if you let the Holy Spirit do His work in you, your thinking will enlarge.

REMEMBER GOD'S BENEFITS

֍ ֍ ֍

We need to be aware that through the Spirit of God we can exercise His benefits, operate in His benefits, be aware of His benefits, walk in line with His benefits and help ourselves. But how many of us are aware of God's benefits in our lives every day?

> **Bless (Affectionately, gratefully praise) the Lord, O my soul; and all that is [deepest] within me, bless His holy name! Bless (affectionately, gratefully praise) the Lord, O my soul, and forget not [one of] all His benefits — Who forgives [every one of] all your iniquities, Who heals [each one of] all your diseases,**
>
> **Who redeems your life from the pit and corruption, Who beautifies, dignifies, and crowns you with loving-kindness and tender mercy; Who satisfies your mouth [your necessity and desire at your personal age and situation] with good so that your youth, renewed, is like the eagle's [strong, overcoming, soaring]!**
>
> **Psalm 103:1-5 AMP**

I'm sure you have read this time and time again. Do you know God's benefits? It doesn't matter whether you are a child or a senior citizen, God is going to satisfy your mouth with good according to your necessity and your desire so that your youth is renewed as the eagle's — strong, overcoming and soaring.

Every day we should remember God's benefits so that we continue renewing ourselves and confessing that which God has given to us. We have to let the Holy Spirit in us do that work so that we are aware of His righteousness. Then we know we have His tender mercies and His loving-kindness working in us and on behalf of us.

REDEEMED FROM DESTRUCTION

෨ ෨ ෨

Not only that, the Lord says He redeems our lives from destruction. He guides us into all truth and guides us in the affairs of life to redeem us from destruction.

Howbeit when he, the Spirit of truth, is come,
he will guide you into all truth: for he shall not
speak of himself; but whatsoever he shall hear, that
shall he speak: and he will shew you things to come.
John 16:13

In order to enjoy this redemption that God has given us by His Spirit to sanctify us or separate us from things that would destroy us (that means injure our health or our peace), we have to let the Spirit of God work in us. We have to learn to walk in the Holy Spirit and to listen to what He is saying to us. He will lead us and keep us in peace and health. To be instructed and reminded by the indwelling of the Spirit is a great provision of our Father God.

And thine ears shall hear a word behind thee,
saying, This is the way, walk ye in it.

Isaiah 30:21

But I say, walk and live [habitually] in the
[Holy] Spirit [responsive to and controlled and
guided by the Spirit]; then you will certainly not
gratify the cravings and desires of the flesh (of
human nature without God).

Galatians 5:16 AMP

To make this possible, we have to walk in the Spirit, and
when we walk in the Spirit, we will not fulfill the lust of the
flesh. That is what the Scripture tells us because fleshly and
human desires, not always, but most of the time, are what
get us in trouble.

When you learn to walk in the Spirit according to God's
plan of salvation, God will speak to your heart by His Spirit
and keep you in His perfect will in all things. The reason we
do not stay in the perfect will of God in all things is because
we do not walk in the Spirit.

Look at what some of the desires of the flesh are:

For the desires of the flesh are opposed to the
[Holy] Spirit, and the [desires of the] Spirit are
opposed to the flesh (godless human nature); for
these are antagonistic to each other [continually
withstanding and in conflict with each other], so
that you are not free but are prevented from doing
what you desire to do.

Galatians 5:17 AMP

desire to do all that is godly, but the
e spirit, and even though you have a
t let the Holy Spirit do His work in you,
ol the flesh, and the flesh will control you.
let the Spirit do His work in us so that we
controlled by the Spirit of God. Then we will
walk .   pirit.

> But if you are guided (led) by the [Holy]
> Spirit, you are not subject to the Law. Now the
> doings (practices) of the flesh are clear (obvious):
> they are immorality, impurity, indecency, Idolatry,
> sorcery, enmity, strife, jealousy, anger (ill temper),
> [Anger here refers to an uncontrolled temper. Never-
> theless, there is an anger that God has placed in you
> for a purpose, and He says be angry and sin not.]
> selfishness, divisions (dissensions), party spirit
> (factions, sects with peculiar opinions, heresies),
> Envy, drunkenness, carousing, and the like. I warn
> you beforehand, just as I did previously, that those
> who do such things shall not inherit the kingdom
> of God.
>
> But the fruit of the [Holy] Spirit [the work
> which His presence within accomplishes] is love,
> joy (gladness), peace, patience (an even temper,
> forbearance), kindness, goodness (benevolence),
> faithfulness.
>
> **Galatians 5:18-22 AMP**

Letting those fruits, by the Holy Spirit, work in you
and grow in you will cause you to walk in the characteristics of God.

We have to learn to walk in the Spirit so that we can be used of God in other things.

> **In [this] freedom Christ has made us free [and completely liberated us]; stand fast then, and do not be hampered and held ensnared and submit again to a yoke of slavery [which you have once put off].**
>
> Galatians 5:1 AMP

We are not to be ensnared to a yoke of slavery, but that is what most of us have done by walking in our own freedom and liberty instead of the freedom and the liberty of the Lord Jesus Christ, and there is a big difference.

> **For you, brethren, were [indeed] called to freedom; only [do not let your] freedom be an incentive to your flesh and an opportunity or excuse [for selfishness], but through love you should serve one another.**
>
> Galatians 5:13 AMP

These verses lead to developing the fruits of the Spirit. They first tell us what we should not do, but what the Spirit of God will do through us. We were called to freedom, but we are not to let our freedom be an incentive to our flesh and an opportunity or an excuse for selfishness.

We need to get our eyes off of ourselves and our problems and what we need to do and what we don't need to do. When we instead get our eyes on God and begin to speak to Him about learning to walk in the Spirit, we become aware of His benefits. That is part of learning to walk in the Spirit and learning to walk in God's plan of salvation for your life. This includes receiving all of the benefits of God who forgives all your iniquities, heals *all* your diseases, redeems your life from destruction, crowns you with lovingkindness and tender mercies, satisfies your mouth with good things and renews your youth so you will soar like the eagles. Hallelujah!

GOD'S BENEFITS IN ME

৯   ৯   ৯

So I can say because I allow the Spirit of God to work within me that I have the benefits of God operating within me. I am aware of them. God has forgiven my iniquities, and if I make a mistake, I can be quick to repent, and He will forgive me. So I am righteous because of Christ Jesus, and because of that, I can walk in divine health. I can know that all the diseases that try to come upon me will have no effect because, through Christ Jesus, I am healed.

I can be aware that every day He keeps my life from destruction. Some dangers I am aware of, some I may never be aware of, but, praise God, because I am operating in God and in His Spirit and in His benefits, I am protected every day. I am kept from destruction.

And not only that, He crowns me with lovingkindness and tender mercies. That means that through His mercy, I don't deserve to get what I get, but I get it because of His mercy. It is one of His benefits. I can know that He is beautifying me and dignifying me and crowning me with those tender mercies and those lovingkindnesses. That is what makes me look the way I look. *His* benefits are what give me my dignity and beautify me. Hallelujah! I like that. And it doesn't matter what age I am, He is going to satisfy my mouth with good things to meet every personal need and desire. He will do it, and He will cause me to be renewed, strong, overcoming and soaring as the eagle.

LEARN TO LISTEN

ဌ   ဌ   ဌ

Those are the benefits of God, and we need to be aware of them and allow them to operate in us by the indwelling of the Holy Spirit. If we learn to listen to the Holy Spirit, at all times He will keep us in health and in peace. If we don't learn to walk in the Spirit, then we won't hear the Holy Spirit, and we will lose out on all of His benefits. In other words, when I live according to God's plan of salvation, God will speak to my heart by the Holy Spirit and keep me in His perfect will in all things.

But how many of us can say that every day we listen to the Holy Spirit and allow Him to speak to us so that we are kept in God's perfect will every day? None of us, I'm sure. But we desire it, right? We should because that is part of learning to walk in the Spirit. When you begin to meditate on the benefits of God, you open yourself up to the Holy Spirit, and you become aware of those benefits. Then you begin to listen to what the Spirit of God is saying to you, so that if sickness tries to fasten itself to you, you can say, "Oh, no you don't. You can't put that on me because I am walking *by* the Spirit of God in the full benefits of God, and one of those is *health!* Therefore, I *will* remain in health."

We need to make ourselves aware every day of the benefits of God and begin to walk in the flow of the Spirit because He is a guide on the inside of us. If you don't learn to listen, what happens? You get born again, you get Spirit-filled, you sit on a pew, you hear the Word of God, but there is no connection or fellowship between the Holy Spirit and your spirit to give you daily directions on how to live according to God's plan of salvation for your life. Then there is turmoil, you begin to have problems with your body, your mind begins to entertain thoughts planted by the enemy, arguments begin at home or at work, strife comes, and then you say, "How did I get in this mess?"

When things aren't going right in your life, check up on the order because God is a God of order. Are you continually renewing yourself in the Word and in prayer so that you maintain your joy and strength? Are you walking in the Spirit so that you live according to God's plan of salvation for your life every day? Are you meditating on God's benefits daily and speaking them forth in your life?

The Word of God is a road map to teach us how to walk, and just going to church on Wednesday night and on Sunday isn't enough! Walking in the Spirit is a *way of life*. It is where your life comes from because He *is* your life. It is in Him that you live and move and have your being. It is a daily walk, a daily renewing, a daily commitment to allow His indwelling presence to guide you.

CHAPTER 6

Establish the Way of the Holy Spirit

§ § §

We have already read what Jesus said in John 14 about leaving the Holy Spirit here on earth when He went back to heaven, but I want to read it again.

> **And I [Jesus] will ask the Father, and He will give you another Comforter (Counselor, Helper, Intercessor, Advocate, Strengthener, and Standby), that He may remain with you forever, The Spirit of Truth, Whom the world cannot receive (welcome, take to its heart), because it does not see Him or know and recognize Him. But you know and recognize Him, for He lives with you [constantly] and will be in you.**
>
> **John 14:16-17 AMP**

This passage tells us just about everything we need to know about the way of the Holy Spirit. It tells us Who He is (Comforter, Helper, Intercessor, Advocate, Strengthener and Standby), what He will do for us (remain with us forever), and how we will recognize Him (the Spirit of Truth constantly living with and in us).

We need to learn the way of the Spirit so that we can see God in all circumstances which form our daily walk with Him. If you look back through your life, you will be able to trace the way the Holy Spirit has worked in your life through certain instances, how He spoke to you, how He ministered to you and the things that happened to you in the spirit realm. But we do not take time to do that often enough. We just think, "Well, praise God, you know, God spoke to me," or "He had that person do this." When we think such thoughts, it is proof we have not established the way of the Spirit in our lives.

These are critical times in which we live. God needs mature people to fulfill His purposes in these final days. God cannot push us into the fullness until we are pure and holy. If we are not walking in the pureness and holiness of God, then we will not be able to stand the move of the Spirit that is coming.

WE HAVE LOST OUR FEAR OF GOD

§ § §

In our minds we want to justify that everything we do is okay. We say, "God knows my heart." It is true that God does know your heart, but that should not be used as an excuse. We, as the Body of Christ, have learned too many excuses so that we can sit back and try to feel comfortable in our walk with God. We think, "I'm okay because nobody else knows."

We have lost our fear of God, and I do not know about you, but I do not ever want to get to that point. I think that is one of the things that has grieved me the most as my husband and I have traveled throughout the United States. Even some pastors have no fear of God.

Some people think, "I can do what I want to; there is always 1 John 1:9, and the Bible says that God's grace is sufficient." These Scriptures are true. They are in the Word of God, but the Bible also tells us to work out our own salvation with fear and trembling. The Bible counsels us about the way we should live and the things that we are to put away. Some of them are from the enemy, but most of them are fleshly. We allow those fleshly things to develop in our lives because we do not continually renew our spirit by the Holy Spirit to maintain the joy of the Lord.

I'VE GOT IT!

§   §   §

There are a lot of people who receive the Holy Spirit and sit down. They think, "Well, I've got it!" I heard a minister tell this story about a man who had been coming to his church for quite some time, and he *finally* got filled with the Holy Spirit. Then he stopped coming to church. The pastor went to visit the man at his home to find out what had happened. The man said, "Oh, didn't you hear? I got it." The pastor said, "Got what?" The man said, "I got the blanket." The pastor was rather puzzled and inquired further, "You got the blanket?" The man responded rather emphatically, "Yeah, you know, the blanket." And then it dawned on the pastor what the man meant, "Oh, the Comforter." The man said, "Yeah, yeah, I got it." The man thought just because he had received the Holy Spirit that was all there was to it, so he didn't think he needed to come to church anymore. This man didn't know the way of the Holy Spirit.

JUST THE BEGINNING

Coming into the fullness of the Holy Spirit is just the beginning of being established in the way of the Spirit. There is so much we need to learn about how He comforts, counsels and helps us, and how He intercedes and acts as an advocate on our behalf and strengthens and stands by us in all the circumstances of our lives. I'll tell you what, the Holy Spirit will stand by you when all else fails. He doesn't run away and hide. He is always there for you just as it says in John 14:26 AMP.

> **But the Comforter (Counselor, Helper, Intercessor, Advocate, Strengthener, Standby), the Holy Spirit, Whom the Father will send in My name [in My place, to represent Me and act on My behalf], He will teach you all things. And He will cause you to recall (will remind you of, bring to your remembrance) everything I have told you.**

Now Jesus was talking here to His disciples because He was getting ready to go away. He has given us His Word, and it applies to everything in our lives as well. He says here that the Holy Spirit will remind us of, will cause us to recall, everything that He has told us through His Word. Not only that, He says the Holy Spirit will teach us all things. So He is saying through the Word of God that there is not one thing in your life that you will come up against that the Holy

Spirit can't teach you. You can then act according to God's plan of salvation, and it will be effective in your life.

ABIDING IN THE WORD

ဖ ဖ ဖ

The sad thing is that if we have not availed ourselves of the Word of God, there is nothing abiding within us for the Holy Spirit to call to our remembrance. There are too many in the Body of Christ who don't ever study the Word for themselves. They just hear Sunday service and Wednesday service and think that is good enough, but that is not what is going to cause them to abide in the Word and the Word abide in them.

To abide in the Word means you have to live in the Word for the Word to live in you. The only way that happens is by getting into the Word yourself every day. If you are in the Word, the Holy Spirit is going to bring to you an understanding of that Word so it remains living in you. This means that in crises, in circumstances, in the every day living of life, there will not be one thing that you go through that the Holy Spirit will not bring to your remembrance, will not recall unto you, will not bring life to you, and cause you to remain in victory every day. But it comes by the Holy Spirit, learning to walk in the Spirit.

KNOWING HIS VOICE

ဖ ဖ ဖ

When you learn to walk in the Spirit, you will *know* the voice of the Spirit. When you hear someone say, "Well, I'm not sure I know the voice of the Spirit," just know that they are not living every day, habitually, constantly in the process of being filled with the Spirit. They are not habitually, constantly in the process of getting into the Word of God and allowing the Holy Spirit to bring to them revelation knowledge that brings understanding so that they can operate in that in wisdom. Because we love the brethren, we need to be bold enough to speak forth the truth to those people in order to bring them out of their nonchalant attitude, their weariness, their fainting.

If you hurt your hand, don't you minister to your hand? Why can't we do that in the Body of Christ? Because we haven't allowed the Holy Spirit to work in us to have the understanding that says, "Hey, that's my brother and he isn't walking in the truth or is hurting, I must restore him and minister to him. He is a part of me." Paul speaks of this in the Scriptures.

> **For as the body is one, and hath many members, and all the members of that one body, being many, are one body: so also is Christ...but that members should have the same care one for another...Now ye are the body of Christ, and members in particular.**
>
> **1 Corinthians 12:12,25,27**

Everyone in the Body of Christ is a member in particular, and they fit somewhere. If we have found our place in the Body of Christ and know what we are supposed to be doing, then we need to be reaching out to our brothers, causing them to come to understanding by the Word in the Holy

Spirit so that they find their place. You didn't do it by yourself, and they can't do it by themselves.

The reason we sometimes struggle and cannot hear His voice is because we are not walking in the Spirit. We have not taken time to fellowship and to let the Holy Spirit work within us so that we know that we know, without a shadow of a doubt. We know His voice, and we do not have to stop and say, "Was that You, God?" We know it was God.

My husband and I have been married over thirty years. Buddy can be on the other end of the earth, but when his voice comes over the telephone, I know it is Buddy because we have fellowshipped for over thirty years. How much more should we know the voice of God and walk in the fullness of it?

When you are full of the Holy Spirit and you know the way of the Spirit in your life, you still need to inquire of the Lord when you believe you are hearing His voice to take action in some specific way. Here is what I mean.

Buddy and I were going on a trip, and as we got in the car, we felt impressed to go a certain way. We talked about it because it seemed silly to go that way since it was two hours out of our way. It seemed like a waste of time. We sat there for a few minutes in the car and discussed it. We were both prepared to take authority over any plan the enemy had to hinder this trip or rob us of our time. However, as we both began to pray in the Spirit, we looked at each other and still sensed that we needed to take this longer route.

When you go to the Father about what you are being led by the Spirit to do, if it is Him, you will still have the same impression because when the Spirit speaks something into your spirit, it is always for a purpose. If it is the enemy, you won't have the same thought or impression.

Anyway, we went the longer route, and here is what happened. We stopped to get something to eat and met some people we had not seen for years. They were in distress, and we were able to help them.

Why does God do things like that? For one thing, He does it for you to realize that you know the voice of the Spirit and to confirm you are learning the way of the Spirit. For another thing, we may have been the closest people He could get to this location to help these people who were in distress. When a prayer needs an answer, God will look for willing servants to do what needs to be done. If we had not been obedient, who knows how long those people might have been in distress.

He Gives Us Peace

ᛸ   ᛸ   ᛸ

Let's go back to the passage in John 14 and continue on.

> **Peace I leave with you; My [own] peace I now give and bequeath to you. Not as the world gives do I give to you. Do not let your hearts be troubled, neither let them be afraid. [Stop allowing yourselves to be agitated and disturbed; and do not permit yourselves to be fearful and intimidated and cowardly and unsettled.]**
>
> **John 14:27 AMP**

Jesus is saying He is giving us His peace. He is saying the world didn't give it to you, and the world can't take it away. Then He says this, **Do not let your hearts be troubled.** *You* is the understood subject of that sentence, is it not? So He is saying, "Because I have left *My* peace with you and because I am peace, *you* should not be troubled or afraid." We can go to Isaiah and see that He is the Prince of Peace.

> **For unto us a child is born, unto us a son is given: and the government shall be upon his shoulder: and his name shall be called Wonderful, Counselor, The mighty God, The everlasting Father, The Prince of Peace. Of the increase of his government and peace there shall be no end.**
>
> Isaiah 9:6-7

When Jesus hung on the cross, He didn't just hang there because of sin and because of sickness, He hung there for peace. Peace means tranquillity of heart *and* tranquillity of mind. So you have to understand that when He hung on that cross, He not only took on all the diseases of the body, He also suffered mentally. That means He suffered every anguish mentally that the Devil would ever try to put on you to cause you to suffer. Why do you think He was unrecognizable on the cross? Because of the anguish, not only physically but mentally, that He went through.

You see, we tend to separate the head from the body, but it is all one — Jesus is the Head, and we are the Body. It is all one. Your head and your body are not disconnected. Jesus suffered so we might have peace. Therefore, we can maintain our peace because He is the Prince of Peace, and He has given it unto us. We have Him on the inside of us.

Therefore, *you* are not to let yourself be troubled or afraid. *You* have to *do* something. Stop allowing yourself to be agitated and disturbed, and do not permit yourself to be fearful, intimidated, cowardly and unsettled. But you don't do it by yourself. You have the Holy Spirit on the inside of you. Allow Him to help you. Allow Him to work in you and help you maintain your peace of heart and mind.

GOD IS LOOKING FOR ACTORS!

Ꙅ Ꙅ Ꙅ

We can't do that if we don't learn to listen to the Holy Spirit because the minute we get a little bit agitated or disturbed, we start letting our mouth go instead of being quiet and listening to the Spirit of God. We become reactors when God has called us to be doers or actors, acting the Word of God, not reactors to situations and circumstances and crises in life. We have the answer. By the Holy Spirit, we can do it. That is part of learning to walk in the Spirit and learning the way of the Spirit.

Jesus was telling the disciples all this to prepare them because He was going away. But for us, He has gone away and come back already. Therefore, He not only dwells within us, but He gave us the Holy Spirit to help us do every thing that He has said in the Word.

We need to let what God is saying to us about learning to walk in the Spirit penetrate our hearts and our minds. We need to see what it all involves. If it is God's plan of salvation to cause you to live right on this earth, that is going to involve a lot, right?

> However, I am telling you nothing but the
> truth when I say it is profitable (good, expedient,
> advantageous) for you that I go away. Because if I
> do not go away, the Comforter (Counselor, Helper,
> Advocate, Intercessor, Strengthener, Standby) will
> not come to you [into close fellowship with you];
> but if I go away, I will send Him to you [to be in
> close fellowship with you].
>
> John 16:7 AMP

That closeness and that fellowship with the Holy Spirit is what causes you to hear Him and causes you to know God's will — what God is saying to you. When Jesus was on the earth, He kept a close communion with the Father. He always spoke what the Father said, not what He thought, what the Father said because what the Father said was right. So by the Holy Spirit, we speak what Jesus is saying to us because He is right because God the Father made Him right. Because we have Jesus in us and He has made us right, then if we hear the voice of the Spirit and obey, we will always operate in that rightness.

Jesus knew how important it was for us to have close fellowship with the Holy Spirit as He says in John 16:8 AMP:

> And when He comes, He will convict and
> convince the world and bring demonstration to it
> about sin and about righteousness (uprightness of
> heart and right standing with God) and about
> judgment.

The Holy Spirit is going to convict you and convince the world about these things through His demonstration. But from where is that demonstration going to come? It is going to come through you — the Body of Christ, the Church — as we read in the next few verses.

> **About sin, because they do not believe in Me [trust in, rely on, and adhere to Me]; About righteousness (uprightness of heart and right standing with God), because I go to My Father, and you will see Me no longer; About judgment, because the ruler (evil genius, prince) of this world [Satan] is judged and condemned and sentence already is passed upon him.**
>
> **John 16:9-11 AMP**

This is why we need to make people understand about judgment. By our own choice, we can come to and be a part of Jesus Christ. He abides in us, we abide in Him, and He is our righteousness. The world needs to know that if they do not make that choice and come into the kingdom of God, judgment falls on them. Not because of them, but because of Satan — *because* Satan is already judged and condemned and sentenced to die. By not choosing Jesus, they are making Satan their father; then they are judged, and the death sentence falls on them as well. By choosing Jesus, we make Jesus our Lord, so we are righteous.

We need to be bold to speak these things when we minister to people so there is clear understanding. We can get understanding from reading this Scripture.

> **I have still many things to say to you, but you are not able to bear them or to take them upon you or to grasp them now. But when He, the Spirit of Truth (the Truth-giving Spirit) comes, He will guide you into all the Truth (the whole, full Truth).**

For He will not speak His own message [on His own authority]; but He will tell whatever He hears [from the Father; He will give the message that has been given to Him], and He will announce and declare to you the things that are to come [that will happen in the future].

John 16:12-13 AMP

Just as Jesus was not able to tell the disciples all that He could have at that time, there are things that He could say to us and into which He could bring us by the indwelling presence of the Holy Spirit; but because we are not ready, He can't speak. He has to wait until we are ready, so we will receive it, and so that it won't affect us adversely.

ARE YOU READY?

⑮ ⑮ ⑮

How often have you heard yourself say, "I don't know why God doesn't speak to me. I don't know why this. I don't know why that." Well, get on your knees before God and He will show you whether you are ready or not. Then have enough sense when God says you aren't ready to say, "Okay, God, what do I need to do to get ready?" And by the Holy Spirit, He will instruct you, through His Word, of what you need to do to get yourself ready for that which you desire or that which you need to know.

The Holy Spirit will guide you into all truth. I don't care what level of maturity you are at, you should always want to learn truth, but don't ever feel because you have moved to a higher level that you have arrived. The Holy Spirit can continually bring you into the knowledge of truth.

NEVER TOO OLD FOR TRUTH!

໑ ໑ ໑

Buddy's grandfather, who was a preacher of the gospel, died when he was ninety-five-years old. About six months before he died, we drove up in front of their house, and he was sitting out on his patio beside the house. He started motioning Buddy to come over to him. He was so excited that Buddy thought maybe something was wrong and hurried over to him. His grandfather had the Word of God in his lap and said, "I want to show you what I learned today."

We are never too young or too old to learn the truth. There is always some new truth to catch hold of that will make us better, that will cause more understanding or enlightenment to bring us closer to the light of God.

The Holy Spirit operates with the whole truth. It isn't His own message or by His own authority; it is directly from the voice of the Father. So when we are listening to the Holy Spirit, we don't speak our own message or by our own authority. We speak the message of the Lord Jesus Christ *in* His authority. He will give the message that has been given to Him, and He will announce and declare to you the things that are to come that will happen in the future.

Then Jesus goes on to say,

> **He will honor and glorify Me, because He will take of (receive, draw upon) what is Mine and will reveal (declare, disclose, transmit) it to you. Everything that the Father has is Mine. That is what I meant when I said that He [the Spirit] will take the**

things that are Mine and will reveal (declare, disclose, transmit) it to you.

John 16:14-15 AMP

So it is by learning to walk in the Holy Spirit and learning His way that the Holy Spirit will give you everything that is in Jesus. It is by the Holy Spirit that you can receive it because He will reveal it, He will declare it, He will disclose it, and He will transmit it to you. He guides your every step helping you to live according to God's plan of salvation.

If you walk in the fullness of the Holy Spirit every day, as we already discussed, there is a joy within you that shows on your face. You are exuberant in the things of God. You do not have up days and down days, but you remain the same because you are walking in the Spirit and learning the way of the Spirit. Therefore, you are confident that your God is like none other, and He will perform His Word in your life when you are doing your part.

When Will We Have More Miracles and Prophecy?

෨ ෨ ෨

People often ask when the prophecy and miracles are going to happen. They will happen when you mature in the Holy Spirit. The power that is coming from the Holy Spirit is so pure that it can only work through pureness and holiness. And the only way that is going to be effective within us is by us walking in the Spirit, maintaining that fullness so that we are walking continually with joy and peace and love.

God has given us gifts, and they are for a purpose. The nine fruits of the Spirit which indwell us help us be more like Jesus. The nine manifestations of the Spirit are for the outpouring of the Spirit. These gifts have two different purposes, but they are both for you. We have tried to use them the wrong way because we did not want to be responsible. But we are responsible.

I am one person, and my head and my body are attached. When you look at me, you don't say, "Well, here is her head and here is her body." You say "There is Pat." Right?

We mentioned this earlier in the chapter, but it is important to reemphasize. Jesus is the Head, and we are the Body. We have looked at them as two separate beings, but the Head and the Body are not separate. They are one, and they should operate as one. Through the indwelling of the Holy Spirit, you learn to operate, performing your part in the Body as one with the Head, the Lord Jesus Christ.

Every day the fullness of the Holy Spirit causes me to walk and flow in exactly what God intends for me, and maturity and the fullness of the Spirit of God comes. God wants to perfect in us His nature through the fruits of the Spirit which bring a maturity, and by the fullness of the Holy Spirit within, He wants to maintain the fullness in continued fellowship.

A Church Without Spot or Wrinkle

ⵡ ⵡ ⵡ

God is calling for a people without spot or wrinkle. He is calling His Church to flow in this day of the Holy Spirit. The wave that everybody is talking about is the way of the Holy Spirit, but there will only be one hero, and He is Jesus.

The Body working together will bring the fullness of the Lord Jesus Christ to this earth.

We are in life-and-death situations every day, and if we do not learn to follow the way of the Holy Spirit in those things, we can give place to the enemy and death and destruction. It is dangerous to be complacent or play games with the things of God.

I have such an urgency in my spirit to get across to you how serious this is and how vital it is that we learn the way of the Spirit. We must learn the way of the Spirit so that we are controlled by the Spirit every day.

We should not wait until a crisis comes to get in the Word and start praying in the Spirit to build ourselves up. We should be built up all the time in the Word and prayer. I pray in the Spirit every day to build myself up. I read the Word every day for the Spirit to bring revelation knowledge to me and to make me what I need to be so that I have knowledge and understanding. Then when opposition or persecution or sickness comes, I can be the same because I let the Holy Spirit work within me. I know His voice, I have studied His Word, and I have knowledge and understanding inside me. Then the work of the Spirit can begin to work in me.

By walking in the Spirit daily, there are five things we attain and maintain: righteousness, fruits, might, revelation and sanctification. We are going to explore these in the next few chapters as we learn more about the benefits of walking in the Spirit.

Walking in the Fruit of Righteousness
❧ ❧ ❧

For we through the Spirit wait for the hope of righteousness by faith.

Galatians 5:5

For he hath made him to be sin for us, who knew no sin; that we might be made the righteousness of God in him.

2 Corinthians 5:21

Righteousness is right standing with God through Jesus Christ. God wants to work out the right standing in your life with right living as the proof of the righteousness of the Lord Jesus Christ. You cannot bring yourself into right standing with good works. You can only do that by allowing the Holy Spirit to teach you how to live right by walking in the Spirit.

A lot of things have been done in the name of righteousness. Some people say "Well, I'm in right standing with God. It doesn't matter what I do or say because I've got right standing with God." Others are always trying to be in right standing with God through their works. That is like standing on both sides of a ditch. They are at far extremes.

WALK IN BALANCE IN THE WORD

§ § §

God intends for us to walk in a balance of the Word by the Spirit of God. We don't need to be in the attitude of "Well, I'm righteous." If you go on doing what *you* want to do and saying what *you* want to say, sooner or later, you take yourself out from under that righteousness. If what you are doing or saying is not according to how He would have you live, then you are not in right standing with God, and you become unrighteous. It is only through asking forgiveness and repenting and coming back into obedience to the Word that you are made right again.

Just because I get born again and Spirit-filled doesn't mean I know how to live right — in that right standing with God on this earth. I can learn how through walking in the Spirit. I can receive that righteousness and maintain it through the Word of God and the Holy Spirit in prayer.

As we previously read in Galatians 5:5, through the Holy Spirit, we wait for the hope of righteousness by faith. We are made the righteousness of God in Christ, but it takes the work of the Holy Spirit to bring that to pass in our natural, everyday lives. Therefore, we must walk in the Spirit to walk out our right standing day by day.

In Ephesians 5:5 AMP, it says:

> **For be sure of this: that no person practicing sexual vice or impurity in thought or in life, or one who is covetous [who has lustful desire for the property of others and is greedy for gain] — for he**

[in effect] is an idolater, has any inheritance in the
kingdom of Christ and of God.

Now that is a pretty strong statement, isn't it? He said,
Be sure of this: that no person.... Many of us define
"impurity" as sexual sin, becoming a drunk, getting addicted
to drugs or something of that nature. And all of those are a
form of impurity. But do you know what the worst impurity
is in your life? It is knowing to do the Word and not doing
it. That is the worse impurity ever in your life because the
Word says it is sin.

> **Therefore to him that knoweth to do good, and
> doeth it not, to him it is sin.**
>
> **James 4:17**

It is those sins of omission that nobody can see, that
nobody knows about that bring the worst impurities in our
lives. Why is that? Because we begin to defeat ourselves
when we say, "Well, nobody knows. I can get away with it.
Nobody knows what I'm supposed to be doing." We forget
that God knows. We convince ourselves nobody knows, and
that makes it okay. We begin to justify it. Then it is just like
the principle in Word of God being applied in a negative
way, line upon line, precept upon precept; we begin to stack
something else on top of that. Then something else comes
and something else, and what happens? We are no longer
walking in the Spirit or doing what we know to do. We are
impure before God. Disobedience is what it is called.

God is calling a mature people in this day, and we have
to have understanding so that we walk knowledgeably in
the wisdom of God. It is one thing to have knowledge but it
is another thing to operate in the wisdom of that knowledge.

And you only do that through the understanding that comes by learning to walk in the Spirit.

A lot of people think learning to walk in the Spirit is some way-out, "floaty" thing out there, like seeing butterflies and silly stuff. That is not it at all. Learning to walk in the Spirit is learning what God is saying to you, living right in this earth because of your righteousness by the Holy Spirit — according to God's will, according to God's plan of salvation — and walking in His will everyday.

> **But I say, walk and live [habitually] in the [Holy] Spirit [responsive to and controlled and guided by the Spirit]; then you will certainly not gratify the cravings and desires of the flesh (of human nature without God).**
>
> **Galatians 5:16 AMP**

Human nature without God? What is that? Human nature without God is carnality — the desires of the flesh. When you do not learn to walk in the Spirit, when you do not learn to live habitually in that atmosphere, your flesh will take over, and you will begin to gratify the desires of the flesh. But if you walk and live habitually in the Spirit, you will not gratify those cravings.

MATURING THE FRUITS IN YOU

ॐ ॐ ॐ

I want to back up and read more of Galatians 5 because all of this has to do with learning to walk in the Spirit, and it is leading up to the fruits of the Spirit. It is telling you all the things you need to do and all the things that you shouldn't do in order to allow the Holy Spirit to mature those fruits in you.

> For you brethren, were [indeed] called to freedom; only [do not let your] freedom be an incentive to your flesh and an opportunity or excuse [for selfishness], but through love you should serve one another. For the whole Law [concerning human relationships] is complied with in the one precept, You shall love your neighbor as [you do] yourself.
>
> **Galatians 5:13-14 AMP**

If you are not walking in the Spirit, you can't do that because you haven't allowed that indwelling presence of the Spirit to mature and develop the love of God in you — God in you Who is love. I like to say it that way because to me these fruits of the Spirit are all attributes or characteristics of Who God is. He is love, joy, peace, patience, kindness, goodness and faithfulness. He is meekness, gentleness and self control. All those are Who God is, and it is through the indwelling presence of the Holy Spirit in your recreated spirit that you can begin to mature in those fruits.

You can walk in love and have joy and peace. You can walk in patience. You can be long-suffering, but not until you allow yourself to practice walking in the Spirit, not until you learn to allow the Holy Spirit to work in you, to mature you into these things so that you no longer look to the cravings and desires of the flesh which is selfishness, but you look to walk in the Spirit, becoming selfless and allowing God to mature you. That is really what it is all about — allowing God to mature us.

Reading further in Galatians 5, we learn that the desires of the flesh are opposed to the Holy Spirit.

> **For the desires of the flesh are opposed to the [Holy] Spirit, and the [desires of the] Spirit are opposed to the flesh (godless human nature); for these are antagonistic to each other [continually withstanding and in conflict with each other], so that you are not free but are prevented from doing what you desire to do. But if you are guided (led) by the [Holy] Spirit, you are not subject to the Law.**
>
> **Galatians 5:17-18 AMP**

And then it tells us what the practices and doings of the flesh are and says they are clear and obvious.

> **Now the doings (practices) of the flesh are clear (obvious): they are immorality, impurity, indecency, Idolatry, sorcery, enmity, strife, jealousy, anger (ill temper), selfishness, division (dissensions), party spirit (factions, sects with peculiar opinions, heresies), Envy, drunkenness, carousing, and the like. I warn you beforehand, just as I did previously, that those who do such things shall not inherit the kingdom of God.**
>
> **Galatians 5:19-21 AMP**

I don't care how righteous you think you are because you received Jesus as Lord, if you continue to operate in these instead of allowing the Holy Spirit to work in you, to begin to mature you into Who God is, you will not have any part in the kingdom of God. The Bible says it right there.

That doesn't mean if you fall and pick yourself up and ask forgiveness and go on with God that you won't inherit the kingdom of God. It does mean that even though you have come into the family of God if you make a habit of continuing to yield to the flesh and to the desires of the flesh and you walk in that instead of habitually learning to walk in the Spirit, you will not be a part of the kingdom of God BECAUSE you can't serve two masters at the same time. You are either serving one or the other. So you are either in righteousness, or you are in unrighteousness. You are either walking in light, or you are walking in darkness.

It all comes back to this — through love you should serve one another. The Bible plainly says that it is because we have passed from death unto life.

We know that we have passed from death unto life, because we love the brethren. He that loveth not his brother abideth in death.

1 John 3:14

That means we have passed from darkness into light through Jesus Christ when we love one another. If we are not loving one another, and if we say we can't love; then we haven't passed from death unto life. It is that simple.

People say, "Well, brother, I'm going to love you by faith." No, you just love him because God loved and because He is love. Don't yield to the flesh. Maybe he hurt you, and you don't like what he did to you. Then he asks for forgiveness, and you say, "I forgive you," but to somebody else you say, "I'm *learning* to love that brother." You may *think* you are learning to love that brother, but you aren't really. Only if you are walking in the Spirit can you love that brother and bring your flesh in line with how you really are and who you really are in the Spirit.

VITAL OR IMPORTANT?

ꝰ   ꝰ   ꝰ

And this I pray: that your love may abound yet more and more and extend to its fullest development in knowledge and all keen insight [that your love may display itself in greater depth of acquaintance and more comprehensive discernment],

So that you may surely learn to sense what is vital, and approve and prize what is excellent and of real value [recognizing the highest and the best, and distinguishing the moral differences], and that you may be untainted and pure and unerring and blameless [so that with hearts sincere and certain and unsullied, you may approach] the day of Christ [not stumbling nor causing others to stumble].

Philippians 1:9,10 AMP

If we are not letting the love of God work in us and come into the full knowledge so that we have keen insight into the things of God, we cannot tell the difference between what is important and what is vital in life. We do not prize what is excellent and of real value, and we cannot distinguish moral differences.

Many people in the Body of Christ do not sense what is vital. They cannot distinguish between moral differences, and they certainly do not prize what is excellent. God and His people should be valued first. If the members of the Body valued God and His people, they would not talk or act in a way that comes against the people of God. People who talk or act this way have not let the love of God abound in them into the full development of knowledge and keen insight into the things of God.

If you ask a person what is vital, the answer is usually, "A roof over my head, or my job so that I can feed and clothe my family, or that I have transportation." But that is not what is vital. That is important, and God is interested in the things that are important, but He is more interested in what is vital.

What is vital is having the complete will of God in our lives on a daily basis so that we can reach out with the outpouring to bring those who are lost, dying and hurting into the kingdom of God. That is what is vital because it is life.

We are living in a life-and-death situation. We as the Body are supposed to be alive unto God, bringing life to a lost and dying world. But we cannot do this without the love of God operating in us because we do not have the compassion for people that we need.

LET THE HOLY SPIRIT BE YOUR GUIDE

๑ ๑ ๑

We need to let the Holy Spirit guide us in everything in which we are involved, because if we do not, we will have a hard time determining when it is simply the attacks of the Devil coming against us or when it is God leading us a certain way for a purpose. Because too many people in the Body of Christ think everything is an attack of the Devil, they do not learn anything from their experiences.

Many times when we let the Lord work in us, the way He works in us certainly is not how we thought it would be. Sometimes it is hard because our flesh wants to have it easy, and we think, "I'm following God. This is going to be easy." It is not always easy, but we have everything within us to remain victorious and not become distressed, defeated and weighed down.

Distinguishing between the important and the vital is necessary in learning to follow the Holy Spirit and in learning His Ways. If you never learn it, you will never recognize when God is working in you, what He desires to do, and how He desires to lead you.

One day I was studying Galatians 5 to teach at a ladies convention. When I got to idolatry, the Spirit of the Lord began to reveal some things to me. I want to share this because I want to stir you up to think about where you are in your thinking in the day in which we are living.

TODAY'S IDOLS!

🝔 🝔 🝔

We think idolatry is what is listed here in Galatians. Idolatry is putting anything else before God. Actually idolatry takes many forms in our society that we don't recognize as idolatry. We get caught up with our bodies. We idolize the way we look. We see it in that Barbie and Ken physique and in all the designer-label clothes and acces- sories we think we have to have. It has become our idol because that is where all of our attention is. Right? Anything that becomes a first priority in your life that is not God is idolatry because you are taken up with that and involved in that instead of with God and your relationship and fellowship with Him.

There are women who idolize their husbands, their children or their homes. It is true, women are to be loving wives, caring mothers and good homemakers. There are just as many men who idolize their jobs, cars or favorite sports. It is also true that men have a responsibility to make a living for their families. It is okay to drive a nice car, and sports provide good exercise and healthy entertainment; but all of these are to be in line with God first in your lives. He is to be first in everything you do and say. If He surrounds you, envelopes you, controls you, and is first in your life; then you have a relationship with Him that is above anything and everybody else. And if that is not so, then whatever you are involved in that takes up all of your time is idolatry to you because that is more important to you than anything else.

Another important issue the Holy Spirit showed me was in the area of rearing children. Parents are raising children with the wrong priorities. We see this all over this country even with pastors. People don't attend church on Sunday night or Wednesday night because Johnny has to be in bed at eight o'clock or they just can't get him out of bed in the morning for school. What is more important in your life? Teaching your child that he has to go to bed at eight o'clock and sleep or learning how to serve God?

The family stays home from church because Johnny has to be in bed by eight o'clock, but everyone watches television and has snacks, and when nine o'clock comes, Johnny still is not in bed. So what is Johnny learning? It is more important that he watches television, is entertained, enjoys snacks and sleeps than serving God and being at the house of God to serve and fellowship one with another. That is idolatry.

Are we really walking in the Spirit? Are we really putting God first in our lives and following after Him? Are we really teaching the moral principles of God to our children? What about just sitting down according to the Word of God and teaching your children the doctrines of Christ so that they have an understanding of salvation, water baptism and communion, so that they know what you believe and why you believe it.

The problem is most of you don't know yourselves. You can't sit down with the Word of God and explain to your child why we take communion or why we have water baptism. You can't say to your child, "Water baptism is a symbol to myself and to everybody that I have been buried with Christ. But praise God, just as He is raised, I am raised in Him. And I walk in that light, in that water, and in that Spirit."

Our kids don't know that. Most of them think it is just another fun thing to do, and we just do it because everybody at church does it. All of this is part of learning to walk in the Spirit because it is learning to live according to God's plan of salvation for your life.

I was raised in church. As a child, I learned to sleep on the pew, and I learned to sleep under the pew, but I was there because I was taught when the house of God was open, you were there. I was taught God was first in your life, and it was important to assemble yourself together with those of like faith who believed like you did and to learn to lift one another up and help and serve one another.

I grew up in an age when the church *was* your life. Everything we did evolved around the church — our parties, our fun — and it was all family. It wasn't that the kids had to do this, and the adults had to do that. We all came together as family and played games, whether they were for the little kids or whether they were for the grown ups. We brought our food and everyone shared with everyone else. We always had a good time.

We never felt like we were left out of anything, and we were fulfilled. Why? Because God had first place in every area of our lives. God was the *center* of our lives. Unfortunately through our intellect, through wanting to look good, through wanting to get across the tracks, many have learned to compromise in today's society.

We must learn to walk in the Spirit so that we know what is moral and discern the difference to know what God is saying to us. Many teenagers today in our churches, our Word of Faith churches, don't see anything wrong with abortion. They say, "Well, it's according to the individual, according to their personal convictions, according to...." You shouldn't have to have a conviction on that. It should never have gotten to that point in the first place. All these things come back to the fact that the Church has failed to continue to walk in the Spirit, learning to walk and to live on this earth in that right standing that Jesus brought to us.

I told you that learning the ways of the Holy Spirit sometimes is not fun. It is a very deep, deep, deep subject. We need to bring ourselves in line with the Word of God and the Spirit of God and live habitually in the Spirit, controlled by Him, so that we operate in the holiness of

God, which first of all is love. When we begin to allow the indwelling presence of the Holy Spirit to work in us and begin to mature us in God and Who He is, our heart becomes His heart, we become as He is, then these other things of the world won't seem important.

People ask me all the time, "How did you do it?" When we started our church in 1978, I was going to Rhema, had three children, helped pastor the church and worked part-time at the office. At one time all three of my children were in three different schools, and I took all of them to school. Then I went to school myself. I cooked dinner and took them to their activities. One of my daughters was a cheer-leader, and I was a sponsor for her squad. My other daughter was on a softball team, and I was involved in that. Our son played soccer and flag football. I can't tell you in the natural how I did all that. I just know that because I was obeying God to the best of my ability at that time, and I was doing everything I knew to do in following what He had told me to do, He took care of me. When you follow through in what He has called you to do, and you have the spiritual laws of God in order and operating in your life, everything will fall in place and work with you and operate with you, and you will get things done.

I can't tell you how I got it done, but it did get done. I cannot tell you that it was always smooth, and there weren't times I was tired. When I went to bed at two and got up at five thirty, it wasn't easy; but I knew God was vital to me, He was my priority, and I knew what He was saying to me, so I did it.

I have not shared this with you to brag on me, but to let you know we all need to have that desire to follow what He is telling us to do no matter what the price. We need to be that diligent and that determined to say, *"God is first place in my life. Therefore, I will walk in the Spirit. I will follow forth with that to which He has called me, and I can do it by the Word and the Spirit of God because I am learning to walk in the Spirit."*

GO WITH THE FLOW

Everybody thinks they have to have a set time and a set place to be spiritual. They get caught up in telling themselves, "I've got to get up at five thirty and go over here by myself and pray. Then I've got to do this at a certain time and all that." I didn't have a regimented schedule, but I always had my prayer time and my study time.

We have to learn to go with the flow of the Spirit. We don't always like what that entails and what that involves, but if we learn to go with it, it works. All this is part of learning to walk in the Spirit. I have experienced it, and I know it works. It is not always just a bed of roses, but because you are learning to walk in the Spirit, you can deal with the distractions and disruptions because you know the voice of the Spirit, and you can hear what He is saying.

The important thing to remember when dealing with distractions and disruptions in life is to keep your priority on God. He is to be your life. When you have within you a burning desire constantly, continually saying, "God is my life. I want to know the heart of God. I want to be as He is," then you can maintain that constant renewal and begin learning to walk in the Spirit every day, living *right* on this earth in that righteousness.

CHOOSE RIGHT LIVING

ဪ ဪ ဪ

We are on our way to living right, but we have to choose to be that way. Some of us don't like to choose because then we are responsible to live up to the Word, but the truth is, we are responsible whether we choose or not. See, that is where we justify things and deceive ourselves. If we don't choose to live righteously on this earth, then we are choosing NOT to walk as God is. He is love, and one step out of love is one step into darkness because we are either going toward life, toward God, or away from Him, toward Satan.

WHAT TOOK ME SO LONG?

ဪ ဪ ဪ

If you practice renewing your spirit and learning to walk in the Spirit every day, then you will get yourself lined up with God's way. In many things you will say, "Why did I take so long? Why didn't I do this before?" Some things with which you have struggled and struggled suddenly won't be a struggle any longer. It takes that determination to learn to walk in the Spirit to see that this is the way of success.

> **Ye have not chosen me, but I have chosen you,
> and ordained you, that you should go and bring
> forth fruit, and that your fruit should remain: that
> whatsoever ye shall ask of the Father in my name,
> he may give it you.**
>
> **John 15:16**

I can't do it within myself because I have not chosen Him, but He has chosen me. Notice in this Scripture the order of what Jesus says. First we are chosen, then we go forth and bear fruit and the fruit must remain, and finally after all this then we can ask anything of the Father in His name and the Father will give it to us. Do you know there are always conditions to the promises of the Word of God? If we learn to walk in the Spirit, we will meet those conditions, so we can freely ask.

It is by this indwelling presence that we begin to operate in the fullness of the fruit, allowing that fruit to work and mature in us. Why? Because the fruit is on the branch, but the life of that branch comes from the inside center core. So, the fruit that comes out and is seen in your life is good when it comes from your inner spirit drawing life from the Holy Spirit inside you. The fruit will never be there if you don't allow the indwelling Spirit to work in you so that you are alive in God bearing fruit that remains.

FRUIT MUST REMAIN

§ § §

When I said you are either walking in light or you are walking in darkness, it is simple — just like a tree. When you cut the branch from the vine, there is no fruit because there is no life, and if you continue to walk in darkness, there will be no fruit because you are separated from God. You are separated from that well, that Spirit that brings life. The further you go in that darkness, the less life there will be in you, and if you remain in that darkness, then as it says in Galatians 5:21, you will not inherit the kingdom of God. If you remain in that "unlife," you will be lost because you can't keep going toward darkness and stay in the light.

The indwelling presence of the Holy Spirit matures the fruit within us and causes it not only to be seen but to remain. It is great when you begin to grow and allow the Spirit of God to work in you and people begin to see fruit in your life, but the greatest thing is when it remains in your life. Jesus said that the first of these fruits is love, and I've already said that is Who God is. He is love. Jesus said in John 13:34-35,

> **A new commandment I give unto you, That ye love one another; as I have loved you, that ye also love one another. By this shall all men know that ye are my disciples, if ye have love one to another.**

I'm afraid that is not what the world has seen in the Body of Christ. Therefore, they have not seen Jesus, and they don't know that we are His disciples because they have seen men's ideas and opinions. They have seen the disciples or the followers of Christ backbiting, fussing, fighting, in strife with one another, running each other down rather than lifting each other up in love, and even saying to another brother who has fallen, "Well, you deserve it. I don't feel sorry for you because you deserve everything you're getting."

LOVE IS NOT AN EMOTION!

৯   ৯   ৯

Well, what about you? You don't deserve to be where you are either as far as looking in the natural. You have not done everything right either. We must understand what love really is. Love is *not* an emotion. Love is a person. Love is a Spirit. Love is God. That is the reason why hate is not the opposite of love. Hate is an emotion which comes from not operating in love. The opposite of love is fear because fear is a spirit, just as love is a spirit. Love is God; fear is Satan.

GOD IS LOVE
YOU ARE LOVE

The first fruit of the Spirit is love. Allow the indwelling presence of the Holy Spirit to mature you in that love. Know that that is who you are; you are love because the Father is love. He plainly lets us see that He is always motivated by that, and He expects us to always be motivated by love, not by selfish reasoning, not by performance. He expects us to honor the Word, do the Word, love one another, uphold one another and serve one another in love by walking in the Spirit.

...Because the love of God is shed abroad in our hearts by the Holy Ghost which is given unto us.

Romans 5:5

What does that mean? It means that the more we pray in tongues and yield ourselves to the Holy Spirit, the more love is being shed abroad in our hearts. We become aware that this is Who God is, and this is who I am. Because He is my Father, and I am born of Him, we know that love is there. It is shed abroad in us. And by the Holy Spirit, we mature in that.

We are love, and we can grow in it by the Holy Spirit, but what have we done with that knowledge? We have let it lie stagnant and untouched. Some people don't even recognize that love is a part of them or that love is a part of God. If love lies dormant within our hearts, we will let our flesh dominate us rather than love dominate us. And I'll say it again, if you are born again and have passed from death into life, then you *want* to love one another. There is a *want to* within you to love one another. If you don't want to, then you haven't passed from death into life yet.

We need to see where we are and how we are operating. Are we truly yielding ourselves to the Holy Spirit so that we are being renewed and so that we are learning to walk in the Spirit? It is possible to retain righteousness, fruit, might, revelation and sanctification. If you are not operating in each of these, then the others are going to be affected. Each one leads into the other.

In other words, if you are not walking in righteousness, then your fruit is certainly not going to mature. And if you are not walking in righteousness and allowing the Holy Spirit to operate in you to mature you in fruit, then when it comes to might, you won't ask for it; and if you do, you may not recognize it or know how to handle it.

As for revelation, if you are not walking in the Spirit, you are not going to hear what the Spirit is saying about the Word and about other things in your life because you won't have your ear tuned. Finally, sanctification only comes by the Spirit of God. All these things are individual, and at the same time they all work together.

I have expounded a lot on righteousness and on fruit, mainly dealing with the fruit of love. Once you recognize that God is love and because you are in Him that you are love, then you will allow that indwelling presence of the Holy Spirit to bring understanding of that and mature you in that. Then the other attributes, or ways God is, will begin to fall in place. If you operate in love, then you are going to maintain joy. And if you operate in love, you maintain your peace. Basically all of the fruits will begin to work in you when you begin to maintain that love element in your life and operate in it.

It also is important to understand that love is not just an attribute of God or Who God is, He also commanded us to *operate* in love. It is a commandment, and if you are not walking in that commandment, then you are not in a position to receive from God.

Fruit *is* the product of our inward life. If we continue to learn to walk in the Spirit, then we will be blessed with results that will be far beyond even our expectations or how we think it should be. God always causes us to triumph and be victorious in everything in our lives. He will give to us in abundance, and we can operate in abundance because He is a God of abundance.

CHAPTER 8

Strengthened by His Might

ⓢ ⓢ ⓢ

May He grant you out of the rich treasury of His glory to be *strengthened* and reinforced with mighty power in the inner man by the (Holy) Spirit [Himself] — indwelling your innermost being and personality.

Ephesians 3:16 AMP

WALK IN YOUR DOMINION

ⓢ ⓢ ⓢ

When we are strengthened with might by the Holy Spirit in the inner man, there is a boldness that comes with that might. That is one of the reasons Jesus told us to ask for boldness. When you ask for boldness, you are asking for the might of the Spirit which will enable you to boldly take your dominion and speak to the enemy. You will boldly repulse him with the Word of God by the Spirit of God because of that might. You won't sit around and take things from the Devil anymore. With that might operating in you, you will stand up and take your ground. You will walk in your dominion.

God has given us dominion in this earth. Through His name and by His Word, He has given us dominion, and if we are not dominating our world, then it is our own fault. I often say, "If you don't like your world, change it." You can change it by keeping yourself renewed, by learning to walk in the Spirit, learning the way of the Spirit, and by doing what you know to do — being a doer of the Word of God.

You can change your world because God created you in His image. He is the Creator. Therefore you have creativity on the inside of you. You can speak forth the Word of God operating in your dominion in the name of Jesus and keep your world as God intended it to be and keep yourself walking in dominion of that world.

A lot of people ask, "What is my world?" It is anything having to do with you — your personality, your home, where you work, where you go, what you do. You can be in dominion if you understand that when you walk in might and in the boldness of the Lord Jesus Christ by the Holy Spirit, there is no reason to be intimidated or to think that you can't speak forth in truth.

YOU ARE RIGHT IN JESUS

ဆ ဆ ဆ

Too often we get hung up in our minds thinking we have to prove that we are right. You don't have to *prove* that you are right. You are *right* because you are in Christ Jesus. You are right because Jesus is right. Jesus never tried to prove that He was right. Why? Because God had made Him right, He just was right. When you receive Jesus and you walk in His authority, in His righteousness, then you are right.

It is selfishness that wants us to try to prove that we are right. Again, we come back to love. When you understand that love is not an emotion, but it is a Spirit, then you can walk in this truth. You can be dominant, but not to the point of dominating because love doesn't *make* anybody do anything. God is love, and His love is unconditional. In 1 John it doesn't say that He came to us because we loved Him, but it says that He loved us first.

In this is love: not that we loved God, but that He loved us and sent His Son to be the propitiation (the atoning sacrifice) for our sins. We love Him, because He first loved us.

1 John 4:10,19 AMP

He loved us, just because He loved us — unconditionally. We weren't good. We weren't doing things just to try to gain His favor. We weren't doing things right. We were a lost and dying generation. But because He is love and because of His unconditional love, He gave His Son, just because He loved us.

LOVE IS STRENGTH

๖ ๖ ๖

You need to understand that in His love is strength, in that is might. The love of God is not mealy-mouthed, wishy-washy, gushy-gushy junk. That is why you can speak the truth in love because it is direct. It is right. You are right, and you have an obligation to speak forth with might and with boldness the truth by the Spirit of Truth, the Holy Spirit.

115

If our motivation is love, then it will not tear down. It will not cut. It will not bring condemnation, but it may bring consecration. You may get your toes stepped on, but if you take heed and take hold, it will lift you up, not tear you down.

We need to see that the love of God, which is Who He is, brings forth that attitude of might and boldness. It comes forth from the inside of you. Until you have experienced it, you may find it hard to understand what I am talking about. I know more about myself than I do anybody else, so I will use myself as an example.

There was a time in my life, not very many years ago, when I was down. I was having a very, very difficult time. People came against us, not only in our ministry, but personally. It is one thing when you do something that causes people to talk, but it is another thing when people come against you because they are jealous, because they don't understand your gift and your calling, because they don't want to receive it, or because the things of God have become commonplace.

BLACK OR WHITE!

֍ ֍ ֍

It was a very hard time for me because I am the type of person that believes either you love God or you don't. I don't have any gray factors. It is either black or white. Everybody is not that way, but that is the way I am. It made me naive in some areas because it is the people that you least expect who come against you, and it is often the people that you have helped the most who turn against you.

116

DO IT FOR THE KINGDOM

ⓢ ⓢ ⓢ

You have to learn the love of God and learn that it is not important what they think or how they perform and that your performance and what you did was not to perform for them or to get goody points, so to speak. What you did was not to exalt yourself and build yourself up, but it was for the kingdom of God. When you learn to operate and walk in the Spirit, then you learn not to take those things personally. Sometimes that is a hard lesson to learn, especially when you have a tender spirit like I do. I am the type of person that just wants to love everybody. I found out that when you operate under the assumption that everybody loves everybody and everything is just going to work for good, you can get really hurt when you wake up and realize that is just not the way it is.

I operate in a prophetic anointing, and people began to talk about me saying that I had a hard spirit and a lot of different things. They didn't respect the gift, and they did not understand the difference between the gift and the person. I began to listen to what they were saying, which was my own fault, and it really caused me a lot of distress. In fact, it affected me to the point that I went into a depression and became ill.

A LOVELINE TO JESUS

ⓢ ⓢ ⓢ

I was in bed a lot of the time, and it was like there was a weight over me. There were days when I couldn't get out of bed. Sometimes a good day for me was to get out of bed and walk across the floor of my bedroom and sit down in a chair. When that happened, I was excited that I had that much energy. The thing that sustained me was my loveline — my love for the Father God and knowing that His love for me was unconditional.

Until you have really experienced that, it is hard to explain and to understand, but that is the substance that helped me — that love from the Father God. There are times when you are your own worst enemy. You do things to yourself. Because of this, I just quit. I just thought, "Well, I'm not going to do this anymore. This is not worth it. If God wants to bring forth a prophetic utterance, personal or otherwise, He can do it through somebody else. I don't have time for this. I don't like it, and I'm not going to do it." So in disobedience I just sat down.

During that depression, I often felt like I was in a deep, dark hole. At the very, very top when I would look way, way, way up, there was just a little pinpoint of light. That tiny little light was my hope because I knew that God loved me, and it didn't matter what condition I was in. He would not let me fall because His love would surround me and would hold me.

LOVE SUSTAINS YOU

𝕾   𝕾   𝕾

A lot of people think it is your faith that sustains you in such circumstances, and it is to a point. However, first and foremost, it is love because your loving relationship with the Father God allows you to operate in faith. The reason people have a hard time operating in faith is because they don't have a relationship with God. You can't exercise your faith if you are not sure about the person in whom you have faith because you don't know him, and you don't have a relationship with him. I knew without a shadow of a doubt that because God loved me unconditionally, His love would sustain me and His love would uphold me. Once you have connected yourself with that love of God, there is a bond that cannot be broken.

During those difficult times, I would pray, and it felt like my prayer would hit me in the face, like it didn't go any farther than the ceiling. Nevertheless, I kept doing all I knew to do. I kept praying in the Spirit, thanking God for His mercy, thanking God for His love, thanking Him that His love would sustain me, and that it was upholding me. I kept reading the Word, even though sometimes when I would read it, I didn't know anymore what I had read than the man in the moon because of that depression. I just did what I knew to do at that time, even when it seemed like I wasn't getting anywhere.

THE LOVE OF THE BODY

🌀 🌀 🌀

This is where we need to recognize how important it is to love one another and to hold one another up with love. It was during that darkest time that I got phone calls. When some people call, it is because they hear something, and they want you to tell them what is going on. But the love of God is when they call and say, "I know you're going through something. It is not important that I know what it is. I'm just calling to let you know I'm praying for you. I want to encourage you to let you know that God has people praying for you because He loves you."

Then I got letters along the same line that ministered to me and let me know that His love was working in my life and that He would uphold me because He did love me unconditionally and would bring me through this.

As I kept doing what I knew to do, even though in the natural it seemed like it was hopeless and it seemed like I was not helping myself, the prayers and love of God's people sustained me. That is the reason we need to recognize that we are a Body, and we are all needed. That is the reason we need to learn to walk in the Spirit so that when the Spirit of God prompts us to pray for somebody, whether we know them or not, we are quick to do it because God would not prompt us if it was not needed, desperately needed, at that time.

I cannot emphasize enough how important it is to have a prayer life that is totally submitted to your Father God and in tune with the Holy Spirit. It is only through daily intimacy with the Father, by revelation of the Word by the Holy Spirit, and by knowing how to hear His voice, that you can immediately know how to pray effectively for someone who is hurting, how to hold them and lift them up as though they are a part of you. It is truly a supernatural act and cannot be accomplished without God's love.

It was because of the love of God that I came through that time, not by any feat that I did. Through His love I came out of that depression a stronger person, speaking with more boldness than I had ever spoken with in my life. When you learn to operate in the love of God and you begin to call on the might of God, that boldness comes. It is stronger than you can imagine if you will be quick to operate in it and obey.

When I am not under the anointing doing what I am called to do for God but just walking around in the natural, I am not a bold person. I am quiet and not a great conversationalist. God has brought me a long way from being very introverted and shy. Now when I stand up in that which God has called me to do, the boldness that comes from within me ensures that I speak the truth.

All of us need to get to that point because we are living in serious times. We must recognize what the love of God really means, what it really is, and Who it really is. It is *God*. When you learn to allow His love to operate in you, there is nothing that you cannot overcome and that you cannot walk in because love is strong. Love is truth, and you *will* speak it forth. When you do, you will be happy and fulfilled and blessed. We must draw upon the Holy Spirit from within us and allow ourselves to be strengthened with that might.

SATAN IS UNDER MY FEET!

§ § §

You must call on that might and be strengthened with that might to repulse the enemy, to have the strength to stamp your foot and say, "Satan, that is enough. You will come no further. You are a defeated foe, and I am victorious. Therefore, you cannot come into my domain. I have authority over you in the name of Jesus, and you are under my feet." Let him know that you know where his place is, and let him know that you are walking in your rightful place. When we learn to walk in the Spirit, we will operate in and attain this might in our lives. So we must get that strength by the Holy Spirit and let that might come forth.

CHAPTER 9

Attain by Revelation and Sanctification

§ § §

But rather what we are setting forth is a wisdom of God once hidden [from the human understanding] and now revealed to us by God; [that wisdom] which God devised *and* decreed before the ages for our glorification [that is, to lift us into the glory of His presence]. None of the rulers of this age *or* world perceived *and* recognized and understood this; for if they had, they would never have crucified the Lord of glory.

But, on the contrary, as the Scripture says, What eye has not seen, and ear has not heard, and has not entered *into* the heart of man, [all that,] God has prepared — made and keeps ready — for those who love Him [that is, for those who hold Him in affectionate reverence, promptly obeying Him and gratefully recognizing the benefits He has bestowed].

Yet to us God has unveiled *and* revealed them by *and* through His Spirit, for the [Holy] Spirit searches diligently, exploring *and* examining everything, even sounding the profound and bottomless things of God — the divine counsels and things hidden and beyond man's scrutiny. For what person perceives (knows and understands) what passes through a man's thoughts except the man's own spirit within him? Just so no one discerns (comes to know and comprehend) the thoughts of God except the Spirit of God.

Now we have not received the spirit (that belongs to) the world, but the (Holy) Spirit Who is from God, [given to us] that we might realize *and* comprehend *and* appreciate the gifts (of divine favor and blessing so freely and lavishly) bestowed on us by God. And we are setting these truths forth in words not taught by human wisdom but taught by the [Holy] Spirit, combining *and* interpreting spiritual truths with spiritual language [to those who possess the (Holy) Spirit].

But the natural, nonspiritual man does not accept *or* welcome *or* admit into his heart the gifts *and* teachings *and* revelations of the Spirit of God, for they are folly (meaningless nonsense) to him; and he is incapable of knowing them — of progressively recognizing, understanding and becoming better acquainted with them — because they are spiritually discerned and estimated and appreciated.

1 Corinthians 2:7-14 AMP

MYSTERIES UNFOLD

ऽ ऽ ऽ

When we walk in the Spirit, we receive revelation knowledge, and by this Scripture we know that the things of God must be spiritually discerned. When we learn that the

Spirit within us is to do a work, then the mysteries of God begin to unfold. We can become better acquainted with them and recognize these truths.

The revelation is going to come by the Spirit of God working within us because it is only by the Spirit of God that we can know the thoughts of the Father. The Spirit searches the deep things of God and brings them forth to us. Therefore, we understand that through the natural man, we are not going to receive understanding from God. It is only through the revelation of the Spirit of God that spiritual discernment comes so that we can go forth in the Spirit of Truth and begin to know the things of God. It doesn't happen by the natural man but by the spirit man, which is the real us.

CULTIVATE HIS FELLOWSHIP

෨ ෨ ෨

When we cultivate our fellowship with the Father through prayer and the Word, we will receive a revelation of the deep things of God by the Spirit if we ask for it. We rob ourselves of the things that God has intended for us to have because we do not fellowship with God and with the Holy Spirit by praying in the Spirit.

John 14:26 says that the Holy Spirit will teach us all things and bring all things to our remembrance. He cannot bring things to our remembrance if we have not studied and applied the Word, if we do not know the Word, and if we have not let Him bring revelation to us as we are studying. The Holy Spirit cannot bring something to our remembrance that we do not know. To know something means we have to have learned it at one time or another.

We need to recognize that we have to be strengthened, that Christ dwells in our hearts, and that we are rooted and grounded in love by the Word and by the Spirit. At the same time, we have to recognize that when we begin to operate in this revelation, we must be careful not to get caught up in what we know intellectually. When that happens, instead of learning and adding to our knowledge of God, we want to make a doctrine out of what we have learned.

STAND ON THE SOLID ROCK

Another pitfall to avoid is trying to establish doctrine based on our own experiences. Everything we do and say must be based on the solid rock of the fundamental doctrines of Christ. Even though certain revelations from the Spirit may come at certain times to help us move into the supernatural so that change and growth begins to come, we must not get carried away with those experiences so that we become unbalanced. The fundamental principles of the doctrine of Christ are where we begin, and that is where we end.

The reason we see so many weird things going on today is because people try to make doctrines based on their experience of some supernatural happening or revelation in their life. Those experiences are all wonderful, but they must not take away from the foundation of Christ. We must stay established and focused on the Rock — Jesus Christ. When we see people trying to be super spiritual or acting weird, we shy away then from walking in the Spirit and being obedient to what God has called us to do because we don't want to be identified with those strange people.

If you are walking in the Spirit of God, then you are not going to act or talk weird. You are going to act and talk like Jesus. At the same time, you must be careful not to deceive yourself by getting caught up in how you look or what somebody might think. Jesus said not to worry about your reputation. It is not important.

What is important is obeying God, following through in the fullness of knowing that God is a real God, and receiving revelation of God's Word by God's Spirit, precept upon precept and line upon line, so that we keep in order and in balance. We must stick carefully to the basics of Christ's doctrine and use common sense.

SANCTIFICATION

๖ ๖ ๖

But we, brethren beloved by the Lord, ought *and* are obligated [as those who are in debt] to give thanks always to God for you, because God chose you from the beginning [to be the first converts] for salvation through the sanctifying work of the (Holy) Spirit and [your] belief in — adherence to, trust in, and reliance on — the Truth.

2 Thessalonians 2:13 AMP

Sanctification of the Spirit is something that many seek. Some believe it is an experience that is to be received once and for all through a season of prayer. That is not what the Word of God says. We need to see how the Spirit is mentioned in connection with sanctification. It says that God has chosen us unto salvation through sanctification of the Spirit and the belief of the truth. The Word teaches us that Jesus Himself was sanctified through the truth and that He prayed that we might be likewise sanctified.

A Never-ending Circle

Some people think that if you pray long enough and hard enough, then you are sanctified. Others think they can be sanctified by their works. The reason a lot of people in certain denominational groups never receive the Holy Spirit is because there is such an emphasis on sanctification. They think that you must first be good enough, then you will receive the Holy Spirit. It is like a never-ending circle for them, but that is the way deception is. It is the work of the Holy Spirit that brings sanctification.

My father once referred to something in a book by Dr. R. A. Torrey which really stuck with me. He said, "We look at Jesus Christ to see what He is and what we therefore ought to be; then we look to the Holy Spirit to make us this that we ought to be."[1]

It is essential that we walk in the Spirit so that sanctification is made possible within us. As believers, we have to recognize that God has His own way of working out His will for our lives. That is the reason it is important that we learn the way of the Spirit.

We "faith" people have gotten so caught up on the victorious side — "I can do all things through Christ," "I am not defeated," and "I am more than a conqueror" that we have become narrow-minded and forgotten about the work of the Spirit within us. The confessions above are true, and we can remain victorious when we go through things, but we have to understand that there are some things that we are going to go through because **the Spirit of God is working out His perfect will in us.**

Let's look at something in Luke, chapter 4, to get a balanced perspective on this.

> **Then Jesus, full of *and* controlled by the Holy Spirit, returned from the Jordan, and was led in (by) the (Holy) Spirit. For (during) forty days in the wilderness (desert), where He was tempted (tried, tested exceedingly) by the devil.**
>
> **Luke 4:1,2 AMP**

Jesus was full of and controlled by the Holy Spirit.

THE HOLY SPIRIT IS WITHIN YOU

၅ ၅ ၅

Buddy and I went through five years of hell, which you may have heard us talk about, but the important thing is what we learned. There were times that we dropped to our knees, but we did not stay there. It seemed as though we were being tossed to and fro, but all the time on the inside of us we had the Spirit of God, and we were letting the love of God work in us. We let the Spirit work through us because we maintained our praying in the Spirit every day to do the best we could to keep ourselves built up. If you face trials and hard circumstances, you can do the same thing when you realize that the Holy Spirit is within you.

The temptations, tests and trials are what will grow you up. The reason a lot of what we call "Word of Faith" people have not grown up is because they sit in churches every Sunday and Wednesday hearing excellent teaching. Their pastor can speak Greek and explain what every word means, but when they leave, they do not even know what they have heard. They say, "Wasn't that good? He is so smart, and he knows the Word of God so well," but they do not know it themselves.

I am not against teachers. We need teachers. They are in the Body of Christ for a purpose. But some of them have become so caught up with their teaching ability that there is no room for the Holy Spirit. Therefore, they have a church full of babies because it takes the Word and the Spirit to grow us up.

Then there are those churches on the other side. All they ever have is a hallelujah time — they dance in the aisles and shout for joy, but they have no Word. They are babies because they do not have the knowledge within them that it takes for them to mature.

In order to grow there must be a balance. We need to have both the Word of God and the Spirit of God to mature us and to grow us up as God intended. Then we will have righteousness, the fruits, might, revelation and sanctification by the Holy Spirit. When we learn to walk in the Spirit, we can attain these in our life, and we can retain them by exercising and walking in them every day.

Finding God in all Circumstances

 identifier identifier identifier

As we learn more about the way of the Spirit in our daily walk, we will be able to more clearly identify how God is working in our lives in all circumstances. We need to recognize that we are individuals, and the way of the Spirit in your life may be different than the way of the Spirit in my life. As we look back at our life experiences, we should be able to recognize where and how the Spirit of God was working with us in situations. In Isaiah 55, it says,

> **For my thoughts are not your thoughts, neither are your ways my way, saith the Lord. For as the heavens are higher than the earth, so are my ways higher than your ways, and my thoughts than your thoughts.**
>
> **Isaiah 55:8-9**

Because His ways and thoughts are higher than yours, and you have not come into full maturity as a believer, you have to realize God has His way by His Spirit working in you to accomplish certain things in your life. What He does will be better for you, will prepare you for other changes in your life that He is bringing you into and will bring growth to your life.

God has His own way of working out His will for your life and for every other individual. That is why we should not question what some people are doing and the way they are doing it. He may just be doing a different work in them and taking them on a different path to get there than He is taking you. This can be true even within your own family. Just be patient and sensitive and let Him work.

LOOK THROUGH HIS EYES

Sometimes, when we are in the midst of difficult circumstances, it is hard to accept or understand His ways, but He always has a purpose if we will just look through His eyes. When the "Word of Faith" teaching first began, people were catching onto it, and there were some who ran with what they *wanted* to hear. There were some who said, "Well, bless God, I've got faith so now I don't have to have any problems. I won't have any tests or trials or temptations because I've got faith in my faith." But that is NOT what the Word of God says.

> **[You should] be exceedingly glad on this account, though now for a little while you may be distressed by trials and temptations, So that [the genuineness] of your faith may be tested, [your faith] which is infinitely more precious than the perishable gold which is tested and purified by fire. [This proving of your faith is intended] to redound to [your] praise and glory and honor when Jesus Christ the Messiah, the Anointed One, is revealed.**
>
> **1 Peter 1:6-7 AMP**

MORE PRECIOUS THAN GOLD

ᔰ ᔰ ᔰ

The Word of God says that the trying of your faith is more precious than gold and that it is through these temptations, tests and trials that the trying and proving of your faith comes. So you had better know that your faith is grounded in the Word of God and that you do have faith in God because you know Him and have a relationship with Him. Otherwise, you really won't know the way the Spirit works in your life. You won't know if it is the Spirit working or the Devil or your own flesh or what. You will be totally confused all of the time because His ways and His thoughts are higher than yours, and He will work things in your life a lot differently than how you think He should.

BE CAREFUL WHAT YOU ASK

ᔰ ᔰ ᔰ

I tell people all the time, "Do not say to God that you want to learn the way of the Spirit in your life, and you want His will to be your will, and you want to know His heart unless you are ready for Him to begin to work." I can guarantee changes will come, and you may find yourself turned upside down and inside out. Some will be fun, and some won't be so much fun because it will be hard on the flesh. Our flesh has a mind of its own and wants to remain like it is. But if you are going to grow in God and learn the way of the Spirit in your life, your flesh and your mind are not going to stay like they are.

Then Jesus, full of *and* controlled by the Holy Spirit, returned from the Jordan and was led in

(by) the (Holy) Spirit. For (during) forty days in
the wilderness (desert), where He was tempted
(tried, tested exceedingly) by the devil.

Luke 4:1-2 AMP

This is when Jesus was led into the wilderness, and it
says, Jesus was **full of and controlled by the Holy Spirit.**
Yet He went through forty days of temptations, tests and
trials. Not only that, it was the Holy Spirit Who led Him
there, so there must have been a purpose, right?

WILDERNESS EXPERIENCES

ॐ ॐ ॐ

A lot of people think they are not going to have
wilderness experiences. I've got news for you. You will. If
you are going to walk through temptations, tests and trials
and come out victorious, there will be some wildernesses in
there. But the key to being victorious is being full of and
controlled by the Holy Spirit.

Because He was full of and controlled by the Holy Spirit in
the midst of His temptation, His test and His trial, Jesus knew
that the Spirit of God was doing a work in Him. He didn't
begin to question, "Why me, God? Why is this happening to
me? What are You trying to do to me?" In that temptation, test
and trial Jesus *remained* full of the Holy Ghost and controlled
by the Holy Ghost and only spoke the Word of the Father.

FOLLOW HIS PATTERN

ॐ ॐ ॐ

Jesus always gives us a pattern to follow. Now if you are
going to learn the way of the Spirit in your life it doesn't

matter what temptation, test or trial you go through, and it doesn't matter whether you are led there by the Holy Spirit for a purpose or whether it is because of the Devil or your own doings. The key is to remain full of and controlled by the Holy Spirit and speak only the Word of the Father.

Always remember that the Devil knows the Word, too. He will come to you and say, "It is written...." That is why you have to know how it is *actually* written because he only speaks lies. He puts enough of the Word in it to get your attention, but then he adds his own lies and deceptions to it. If you don't know the truth and if you don't know the Spirit of Truth, you will be deceived instead of remaining full of the Holy Spirit and speaking the Word of the Father.

DON'T SIT DOWN TOO SOON

ᦙ ᦙ ᦙ

I want you to see what else it says at the end of Jesus' encounter with the Devil.

> **And when the devil had ended every [the complete cycle of] temptation, he left Him — temporarily, that is, stood off from Him until another more opportune *and* favorable time.**
>
> **Luke 4:13 AMP**

Often when we win a victory, we rejoice and shout and sit down. You must understand that the Devil may have finished this temptation, and he will leave you temporarily, but it won't be long until there will be another opportune, favorable time. The Devil does not give up easily, and he will always come back for another try.

Don't wait until you are in the midst of the battle before you begin to speak the Word and pray in the Spirit. The key to it is to keep yourself full of the Word every day. Keep yourself full of the Spirit of God so you are full of and controlled by the Spirit every day whether you are in a temptation, test and trial or whether you are walking in victory at the time. Be ready at all times, and there will be fewer and fewer opportune and favorable times for the Devil to come back with his harassment.

Then Jesus went back full of *and* under the power of the (Holy) Spirit into Galilee.
Luke 4:14 AMP

Notice that this verse begins with the word, "then." Every word in the Scripture is significant. The "then" was *after* all forty days in the desert and all the temptations, tests and trials were put before Him by the Devil. Jesus went in full of and controlled by the Holy Spirit, and He knew He was led there by the Spirit because He knew the way of the Spirit in His life. He knew that it was critical for Him to go through this, not only to be strong, but to maintain what He was here on this earth to do, to carry out His Commission. You are here on this earth to carry out His Commission. All the things that cause you to waver in your faith or all the things that cause you not to walk in the Spirit, not to learn the way of the Spirit, are distractions to prevent you from keeping your eyes on Jesus, speaking the Word, and being full of and under the power of the Holy Spirit so that you can complete the Commission that has been given to you. Some of us have even forgotten what that Commission is, and some of us have never known what it is.

The last part of Luke 4:14 AMP says, **and the fame of Him spread through the whole region round about.** When we have come through a temptation, test and trial how many of us have had someone jump up and say, "Oh, look at her. She went through that temptation, test and trial, and look at her rejoicing. She is still full of the Holy Spirit." No, most of the time somebody comes up to you and says, "Well, what's the matter? It'll be okay," or else they join in with you and say, "Oh, you poor thing."

Jesus came through His temptation, test and trial and *remained* full of the Holy Spirit, controlled by the Holy Spirit, and full of His Father because He kept His eyes on Truth. He listened only to the Spirit of God. Therefore, He remained victorious, and He went out doing the work of the Father, teaching and admonishing the ones that came to hear, healing the sick, setting the captives free, proclaiming the acceptable year of the Lord.

What do we do? We sit down and say, "Whewww! I'm glad that's over." We need to learn the way of the Spirit. It is good that it is over, and we have excelled. We hope we have grown through that temptation, test and trial. We know God, and our faith is working, and all that is good. However, the most important key in all this is remaining full of the Holy Ghost and speaking forth the Word of God, at all times, under all circumstances, under all situations, no matter if they are good or bad.

COMING INTO DEEP PLACES

ⓢ ⓢ ⓢ

Some of the hardest tests in your life will be God leading you so that you come into the deepest places with Him. I shared with you my experience with depression. It was His love that carried me through. I went into the deepest places with God, and I came out of that with strength, knowledge, understanding and wisdom. I came out walking in that knowledge and wisdom, not allowing any of those things to affect me any longer, remaining full of the Holy Ghost, and speaking the Word of the Father.

We need to understand that it is not always the Devil putting us in a hard place. Sometimes it is the Holy Spirit putting us in that hard test so that we come into that deep place with God. But most of the time, when we get in the hard place, rather than running to God and going into Him and into that deepness with Him, we run to somebody, "I need help. You've got to help me. Oh, Pastor, pray for me."

You don't always recognize that it is the Spirit of God working within you to bring you into a deep place with God because He is getting ready to promote you. He is getting you ready for change. We don't move from one place to another with God without growth and change and without God by His Spirit working in us and affecting us.

NOT ABOVE OUR MASTER

Jesus suffered tests and trials, and the Bible says we are not above our master, and He is our Master. We need to know that if He is the Head and we are the Body, then we are going to go through a lot that He went through. But see, He is the perfect example. He is the example to show us that He has given us His Word and the Holy Spirit, and that was all that He had.

He is here to tell us, "By My Spirit and by My Word, you can be like Me. You can remain victorious. You can have might and boldness. You can walk in righteousness and in revelation knowledge. You can have the fruit remain within your life and at the same time go through these things and not be scarred or downhearted but stand up strong because I made it through." He has given us everything that He had — the Holy Spirit and the Word of His Father — and if He can do it, then we can do it.

Now we must learn how the Spirit of God works in us by looking back at our experiences and tracing God in those experiences so that we can see whether it was God or the Devil. So that we recognize the way in which God works with us, by His Spirit, in motivating us and maneuvering us and getting us in position to grow and to operate in the fullness of the Holy Spirit in the Word of God. Hebrews 2:18 AMP says,

> **For because He Himself [in His humanity] has suffered in being tempted (tested and tried), He is able (immediately) to run to the cry of (assist, relieve) those who are being tempted *and* tested *and* tried [and who therefore are being exposed to suffering].**

Because He suffered, He will run to us when we call upon Him to help us in our suffering. He will give us His Word as He has given us the Holy Spirit. Therefore, we can allow that Spirit and His Word to work in us and help us in our time of trial and temptation.

Hebrews 4:15 AMP says,

> For we do not have a High Priest Who is unable to understand *and* sympathize *and* have a shared feeling with our weaknesses *and* infirmities *and* liability to the assaults of temptation, but One Who has been tempted in every respect as we are, yet without sinning.
>
> Let us then fearlessly *and* confidently *and* boldly draw near to the throne of grace — the throne of God's unmerited favor [to us sinners]; that we may receive mercy [for our failures] and find grace to help in good time for every need — appropriate help and well-timed help, coming just when we need it.

We have a High Priest Who has been touched with all of the infirmities and all of the temptations that we will go through, but He did not sin. We can come boldly to Him because He can relate to us, and we can relate to Him, and there is victory in going to Him. But so many times in our temptations, tests and trials, we run from God rather than to Him. That is why we don't get help in the time of need.

Suffering came from without to Jesus, instigated primarily by the Devil. But know this, God's Spirit has to be in a human being to operate. Satan duplicates everything God does, so the Devil has to be in a human being the same as God is to operate. The Devil will try to come into you to operate so that you will do the opposite of what God intended. He will begin to come against you and buffet you. Just remember, you have the Spirit of Truth in you and the Word of God to keep you in line. You do not have to succumb to the Devil's lies, threats and temptations. Hebrews 5:2 says,

> Who can have compassion on the ignorant, and on them that are out of the way; for that he himself also is compassed with infirmity.

Acts 5:41 AMP says,

> So they went out from the presence of the council (Sanhedrin), rejoicing that they were being counted worthy — dignified by the indignity — to suffer shame *and* be exposed to disgrace for [the sake of] His name.

Jesus suffered shame, right? So, why are we so afraid of suffering shame? We are not above our Master. We should rejoice that we are counted worthy to suffer shame for His name. So what if somebody talks about you. They are going to find something to talk about anyway. Don't take it personally. We have to get to that point. But we can only get to that point when we are full of and controlled by the Holy Spirit. Otherwise, we are still walking in our selfish, carnal, natural mind, and it causes our flesh to rise up. We say, "Did you hear what they said about me? What they did to me? I just can't forgive them," or else we say, "I forgive them, but I can't forget it." That is not scriptural, and it isn't the way of the Spirit.

LET THE PAST BE PAST

§ § §

There are a lot of people who may have suffered abuse as children or had difficult lives, and they use it as an excuse for having pity parties, for feeling sorry for themselves, and for living in anger and bitterness. The Bible says that when

141

you come to Jesus, He frees you from all of the past. The past is past, and He brings you into His liberty.

I don't care what has happened to you or when it happened to you. When you come into Jesus Christ, there is nothing that cannot be taken away from you and lifted from you. But many people hang onto these past hurts because they want sympathy. They don't want to have to do anything about it, and hanging onto those past hurts is their excuse for not following God or for not being strong in God.

Here is what you will hear them say, "You just don't know what I've had to go through." That is true, but they haven't had to go through anything close to what our Lord and Savior went though. They haven't had to die and shed their blood for the sins of the entire world. What I'm saying to you is that no matter what painful or horrible experiences you have gone through in the past, you do not have to walk in those kinds of bondages any longer. Jesus suffered so that you can walk in freedom.

If you don't learn to walk in the Spirit and learn the way of the Spirit in your life, you won't let go of those things of the past. You must let go of them and *let* the Spirit of God work in you to pull all that pain out and free you. As you learn to walk in the Spirit, you begin to operate in the love of God and that junk from the past won't stay. All those hurts, all those feelings can't stay in you because the love of God is pure. It is a "white-heated" love.

TRIED BY FIRE

๑ ๑ ๑

Do you know what "white-heated" means? Have you ever seen on TV how gold is melted down until it can be poured into molds to form it into whatever shape is desired? The fire that is hot enough to melt gold is a "white-heated" fire. It is hot!

When we were in South Africa, we went down in a gold mine, and the workers showed us how it was done. We were standing way, way back away from them, probably thirty feet or more, and we still could feel the heat from the furnace. They used a very long, arm-like apparatus to take the liquid gold out of the heat and pour it into forms to make gold bricks. When we stood up closer so we could see what they were doing, it was extremely hot. The workers stood quite a ways from that furnace, but they had on insulated clothing because it was so hot. That is how hot a white-heated fire is.

When you are tried with that kind of a fire, you are going to come out pure, but it isn't going to be fun. It is going to be hot, but my Bible says when we are led through the fire, we won't be burned, and when we go through the water, we won't drown. Hallelujah!

> **When you pass through the waters, I will be with you, and through the rivers, they will not overwhelm you. When you walk through the fire, you will not be burned or scorched, nor will the flame kindle upon you.**
>
> **Isaiah 43:2** AMP

Notice in this Scripture it says, **when you pass...** it doesn't say "if you pass...." That means we are going to have times of testing, trials and temptation because this is the way the Holy Spirit works in us to purify us, to bring us into that next level of wisdom, that next level of knowledge, to bring us into that place into which He is getting ready to move us for promotion or whatever our next level is to be.

It is not as we choose but as He says. He is the only one Who knows our hearts, and He is the only one Who knows when we are ready for promotion. Sometimes, by the Spirit, He will reveal that promotion to us if we are mature enough to handle it and not run off with it. However, when God begins to speak to us, what do we do most often? We have to run and tell somebody, and then it gets all messed up.

Just as Jesus suffered, we can read how the apostles also suffered in the early days of the Church. When the Lord spoke to Ananias to go and lay hands on Saul (later named Paul), He foretold how Saul would suffer in His name.

> **But the Lord said to him, Go, for this man is a chosen instrument of Mine to bear My name before the Gentiles and kings and the descendants of Israel; For I will make clear to him how much he will be afflicted *and* must endure *and* suffer for My name's sake.**
>
> Acts 9:15-16 AMP

This same Paul also speaks of the suffering required of Christians.

> **But in all things approving ourselves as the ministers of God, in much patience, in afflictions, in necessities, in distresses, In stripes, in imprisonments, in tumults, in labours, in watchings, in fastings.**
>
> 2 Corinthians 6:4-5

I don't think there are very many of us that have really been in prison because of God or because of the Word of

God. I know people in other countries that have, but not in this country.

PAUL'S HARDSHIPS

If you think you have it tough, look at what Paul went through! Paul states:

> Are they ministers of Christ? (I speak as a fool) I am more; in labours more abundant, in stripes above measure, in prisons more frequent, in deaths oft. Of the Jews five times received I forty stripes save one. Thrice was I beaten with rods, once was I stoned, thrice I suffered shipwreck, a night and a day I have been in the deep;
>
> In journeyings often, in perils of waters, in perils of robbers, in perils of mine own countrymen, in perils by the heathen, in perils in the city, in perils in the wilderness, in perils in the sea, in perils among false brethren; In weariness and painfulness, in watchings often, in hunger and thirst, in fastings often, in cold and nakedness. Beside those things that are without, that which cometh upon me daily, the care of all the churches.
>
> 2 Corinthians 11:23-28

Paul toiled in hardships while watching often through sleepless nights. Besides going through all the hardships that came against him externally, Paul still had the pressure and responsibility to see that the churches for which he was responsible were getting what they needed and being cared for as they should. He came through because of the attitude of his heart. He did not give up and say, "If it weren't for the people, we could make it."

CAST DOWN BUT NOT DESTROYED

It has often been said that we are our own worst enemies. We do not have half the things with which to cope that Paul did. This shows us how easy we really have it, and yet we still complain.

The Word tells us that we must suffer with Jesus that we may be glorified together because we are heirs and joint-heirs with Him, and that glory shall be revealed in us. But it is not going to be revealed in us if we don't suffer with Him.

> **And if children, then heirs; heirs of God, and joint-heirs with Christ; if so be that we suffer with him, that we may be also glorified together. For I reckon that the sufferings of this present time are not worthy to be compared with the glory which shall be revealed in us.**
>
> **Romans 8:17-18**

We must stay God-focused and see through His eyes to comprehend His glory. Then whatever temptations, tests or trials we go through, it won't matter because it is not what we are going through that is important, it is what it is doing to mature us and grow in us so that the glory of God will be revealed in us. That is the ultimate.

If Jesus can say all that He went through was worth it — to give up His life so that we can be saved, be sons of God, be heirs of God, and joint-heirs with Him — how much will it be worth for us to go through that white-heated, fervent heat of God to work in and through us by His Spirit so that ultimately the glory of God shall be revealed in us? It is worth it, and we can bear it all if we put our trust not in ourselves but in God who has delivered us from death.

> **For we preach not ourselves, but Christ Jesus the Lord; and ourselves your servants for Jesus' sake. For God, who commanded the light to shine out of darkness, hath shined in our hearts, to give the light of the knowledge of the glory of God in the face of Jesus Christ. But we have this treasure in earthen vessels, that the excellency of the power may be of God, and not of us.**
>
> **We are troubled on every side, yet not distressed; we are perplexed, but not in despair; Persecuted, but not forsaken; cast down, but not destroyed; Always bearing about in the body the dying of the Lord Jesus, that the life also of Jesus might be made manifest in our body. For we which live are alway delivered unto death for Jesus' sake, that the life also of Jesus might be made manifest in our mortal flesh. So then death worketh in us, but life in you.**
>
> 2 Corinthians 4:5-12

We may be tossed on every side, but we will not be distressed if we let the Holy Spirit have His way and work in us. We may be perplexed, but we will not despair. We may be persecuted, but we will not be forsaken. We may be cast down, but we will not be destroyed.

The types of temptations, tests and trials may be different from what Paul went through or different for each of us, but we have the same God and are dealing with the same Devil. There is nothing new under the sun, and what goes around comes around. Just remember the Devil is a liar and the father of lies. There is nothing he can bring against you that he has not already tried against Jesus, and Jesus overcame.

We worship God Who is the God of Truth. So, why should we listen to the Devil who is the father of lies? I once heard a pastor say this, "Here is how you can tell the Devil is lying — when his lips are moving!" We know by now that anything he says is a lie, so why even listen to it?

It doesn't matter through whom the Devil's lies are spoken. That is how he hurts us. Nine times out of ten, his lies come through the lips of brothers and sisters in the Lord or even the lips of family members. We have to learn to rise above that.

In Jesus' day, it was the Pharisees, the religious people who came against Him. It is no different today. Religious people are going to come against you because they don't like the Truth. They want to operate in their own parameters of how they think things are. If you get outside of that, then you are wrong in their eyes. If you speak the Word of God, it is Truth, and you don't have to prove you are right. Jesus made you right. Just let them go their way and pray for them. If you don't learn the way of the Spirit in your life, you will stay upset and offended all the time. All that does is hinder you from walking in the fullness and going forth to complete the commission He has given to you.

**From henceforth let no man trouble me: for I
bear in my body the marks of the Lord Jesus.**

Galatians 6:17

MARKED BY PERSECUTION

๖ ๖ ๖

Paul had marks on his body where he had suffered not from sickness and disease but from persecution. He had been stoned and beaten. He had been in prison with his hands and feet in stocks. We have not experienced that kind of persecution today in America, but it is happening in greater measure in other places in the world.

What man may use to come against us is not important. We have the Lord Jesus Christ; we have suffered with Him. We can rejoice and be glad because we have an opportunity for our faith to grow and be strong, and, at the same time, learn the working and way of the Holy Spirit of God. Then God's perfect will can always be accomplished in our lives.

WALK IN OBEDIENCE

๖ ๖ ๖

In some situations today, occasionally we are seeing people go to jail, but often it is because they are not walking in the confines of the law. When some of the abortion protesters apply for permits, they are given a permit which has certain parameters attached. When they don't abide by those parameters, then they are arrested and put in jail. It has nothing to do with standing up for what they believe, it is because they disobeyed the law. We must have enough sense to obey the laws of the land and the Word of God.

COUNT IT ALL JOY!

֍ ֍ ֍

We have more freedom in our country than in most countries. But even when we do face persecution, we cry and carry on saying, "I don't know why this is happening to me. I was just trying to do what God said." The Word says we are to rejoice in times of temptation, testing and trial.

> **Count it all joy when ye fall into divers temptations; Knowing this, that the trying of your faith worketh patience.**
> **Blessed is the man that endureth temptation: for when he is tried, he shall receive the crown of life, which the Lord hath promised to them that love him.**
>
> **James 1:2-3,12**

Look at what is happening in your life. Look at the way the Spirit is working. Rejoice knowing that the trying of your faith is better than gold, knowing that you are not above your Master, knowing that there is nothing you are going through that He didn't suffer. He suffered more extensively than we ever have.

Our humanistic society is trying to take Christianity out of the schools. It is okay for those in other religious and secular groups to speak up, but not for Christians. Why? Because they don't want to hear the truth. Satan always comes against the truth. It is time for Christians in America to wake up and speak up for what is right. When your neighbors or coworkers or school officials come against you, don't take offense by taking it personally. Just speak the truth.

HOLD FAST TO THE WORD

❦ ❦ ❦

No matter how many persecutions came against Him, Jesus always stayed true to the Word and Spirit. We need to live with the same determination. Not staying true to the Word and the Spirit has been the downfall of many people. When the persecution comes, we begin to look at the persecutions and not stay true to the Word and the Spirit.

Often, the only time we start to fight the good fight of faith and pray in the Spirit and build ourselves up is when we are in trouble. But we are supposed to remain the same in trouble or out of trouble.

REMAIN THE SAME

❦ ❦ ❦

Remaining the same means that instead of allowing ourselves to be overcome by bad circumstances, we continually speak the Word and pray in the Spirit to stay on the same spiritual level all the time. It means not letting those bad circumstances pull us down as we do many times basically because we do not stay full of the Holy Spirit and listen to God as He is speaking to us. What gets us in trouble is that we do not remain the same.

**Yet if any man suffer as a Christian, let him not
be ashamed; but let him glorify God on this behalf.**

1 Peter 4:16

We need to abstain from fleshly lusts which war against our spirits and our souls. The only way we will be able to do that is by learning the way of the Spirit.

Jesus did not sin by getting into disobedience. Disobedience is what leads us into the fleshly, carnal sins. We often relate sin to adultery, fornication and drunkenness. Jesus was tempted in every manner that we are tempted but He did not fail to obey, because disobedience is sin. In every temptation and in every trial, He did exactly as He was told to do by the Spirit of God. He kept His eyes on the Father, listened to the Spirit and did what He heard. We need to follow His example and keep our eyes on Him, listen to the Spirit and do what He tells us to do.

Our Walk Is Serious

 followed by decorative marks

A big problem in the Body of Christ is that many people have not walked in an upright manner before God and man. The lack of fear of God and reverence for Him that Buddy and I have seen as we have traveled around the country has amazed us. It is sad. Everything is fun and games. These are strong statements, but we need to hear them and take heed.

The things of God are serious business. We need to remember that these things are a matter of life and death — not only for us but for others. The Devil is out to steal, kill and destroy!

We must take the temptations, testings and trials that come our way seriously, no matter where they come from. We must live godly lives, seek God in all circumstances, and allow the Holy Spirit to purify and mature us so that we can walk uprightly before God and man and glorify the Father in all that we do.

CHAPTER 11

The Freedom of the Truth

🔿 🔿 🔿

The freedom that the knowledge of the truth of the Lord Jesus Christ and His Word has given to you should be more important than any persecution or hardship with which you come in contact. Colossians 1:24 says,

> **Who now rejoice in my sufferings for you,
> and fill up that which is behind of the afflictions
> of Christ in my flesh for his body's sake, which is
> the church.**

In all of the persecutions and hardships that Paul faced, he stayed true to the call of God, to walking forth in the truth because the freedom of that truth was more important to him than any persecution that he could ever suffer. That is the way you need to see it.

A PRICE AND A REWARD

🔿 🔿 🔿

There is a price for speaking truth, and there is a reward. Here is what the Word says.

If we suffer, we shall also reign with him: if we deny him, he also will deny us.

2 Timothy 2:12

If we suffer with Him, we will actually reign with Him. That is an awesome promise to hold in our hearts. But don't get so excited that you don't look at the rest of the verse. Do you know that when you do not stand up and speak the truth, you are denying Jesus? We must wake up, listen to and walk in the Holy Spirit, learn the way of the Spirit in our lives so that we live godly.

LIVING GODLY IN CHRIST

Yes, even when we live godly lives, we will suffer persecution.

Yea, and all that will live godly in Christ Jesus shall suffer persecution.

2 Timothy 3:12

Does it not tell us that when we began to take hold of the truth of the Word that we would be persecuted? Anytime you stand up for truth and you are a doer of that truth, there is persecution that is going to come because people won't like it. They don't like it that you are blessed because of the truth. We need to understand that and not take it personally. Those that **live godly in Christ Jesus shall suffer persecution.**

When we recognize this is the truth of God's Word, then we won't let that opposition or that persecution bother us. Like I said before, it hurts a lot of times when it comes from fellow Christians, but you won't let it bother you if you are living godly in Christ Jesus. Don't get sidetracked because you get persecuted or talked about and think, "Well, maybe I missed it somewhere because they are saying this and they are saying that." No, more than likely, they are saying what they are saying because you are speaking the Truth. If you are living godly, you will know the Truth.

Learn the way of the Spirit in your life because sometimes He leads us in these ways to strengthen us, to cause change to come in us which causes growth and prepares us for what lies ahead. I don't know about you, but I don't want to stay where I am. I want to go up higher. I am willing to learn the way of the Spirit and allow how He works in me to cause that growth and that change so that I'm prepared and ready to go up with Him. The key is living godly. That way you will know when persecution comes, you will know the truth, and you won't take the words others say personally. You will just keep on moving in the Spirit, going higher with God.

We read in James that we are to count it all joy when we face trials, temptations or persecution. That sounds strange in the natural, but we can do it because we know that each trial or test is going to cause growth. If we remain full of the Spirit, walking in the Spirit and speaking the Word, we can endure. Then as we are steadfast, God will have His perfect work in us.

SEEK HIS WISDOM

§ § §

If you don't know what is going on or don't understand how to deal with it, ask Him, and He will tell you. The reason we don't ask is that we don't even recognize that it is the Spirit of God. Just because it is something we don't like, then we think it has to be the Devil. That isn't always true. So, if you lack wisdom, ask Him.

> **If any of you is deficient in wisdom, let him ask of the giving God [Who gives] to everyone liberally and ungrudgingly, without reproaching or faultfinding, and it will be given him.**
>
> **James 1:5 AMP**

It will be given to you when you ask. Of course, you must ask in faith and then not waver in your faith, not hesitating, and not doubting. Humble yourself in that circumstance so that you will be called into the true riches and be an heir of God. See yourself as an heir of God.

It says in 1 Peter 3:14-17 AMP:

> **But even in case you should suffer for the sake of righteousness, [you are] blessed — happy, to be envied. Do not dread _or_ be afraid of their threats, nor be disturbed [by their opposition]. But in your hearts set Christ apart as holy [and acknowledge Him] as Lord. Always be ready to give a logical defense to anyone who asks you to account for the hope that is in you, but do it courteously and respectfully.**
>
> **[And see to it that] your conscience is entirely clear, so that, when you are falsely accused as evildoers, those who threaten you abusively _and_ revile your right behavior in Christ may come to be ashamed [of slandering your good lives]. For [it is] better to suffer [unjustly] for doing right, if that**

should be God's will, than to suffer [justly] for doing wrong.

That is how most of us suffer, for doing wrong. When we are talked about, we don't like it because often it is justified. Paul said it is better to suffer unjustly for doing right than to suffer justly for doing wrong. The main thing you need to do is to be sure that your conscience is clear so that when they falsely accuse you, they will come to be ashamed for slandering your good life. That is what happened with Jesus. They came to be ashamed because they falsely accused Him.

TAUGHT BY DEMONSTRATION

We don't like to think this, but there are some instances when God talks to us through His Word and by His Spirit, and we don't listen. So, He teaches us through demonstration. We say we want His will done in our life, and He is seeing to it that His will is going to be carried out even if it means having to suffer.

PERSECUTION IS *NOT* SICKNESS

We need to understand that such suffering is from persecution and opposition, not from sickness and disease. You never read in all the persecutions of Christ when He walked on this earth doing what God told Him to do that He was ever sickly or diseased. The only time that came upon Him was when He was on the cross so that we could be free from it.

We need to have a dying-to-self experience because that is what Jesus did really. He died to self so that we might be free. When we die to self through Jesus Christ, He makes us free. But we have to die to self daily to remain free because our carnal nature and our carnal thinking will bring us back into bondage.

Selfishness will bring you back into bondage by getting you off track, out of walking in the Spirit, and out of growing in God. When you are hung up on yourself, you suffer from the "I wants" and "what about me" syndrome. You never heard Jesus speak those words because He was not selfish.

First Peter 4:12-16 AMP says:

> Beloved, do not be amazed and bewildered at the fiery ordeal which is taking place to test your quality, as though something strange — unusual and alien to you and your position — were befalling you. But in so far as you are sharing Christ's sufferings, rejoice, so that when His glory (full of radiance and splendor) is revealed you may also rejoice with triumph — exultantly.
>
> If you are censured *and* suffer abuse [because you bear] the name of Christ, blessed [are you] — happy, fortunate, to be envied, with life-joy and satisfaction in God's favor and salvation, regardless of your outward condition — because of the Spirit of glory, the Spirit of God, is resting upon you. *On their part He is blasphemed, but on your part He is glorified.*
>
> But let none of you suffer as a murderer, or a thief, or any sort of criminal; or as a mischief-maker (a meddler) in the affairs of others — infringing on their rights. But if [one is ill-treated and suffers] as

**a Christian [which he is contemptuously called], let
him not be ashamed, but give glory to God that he
is [deemed worthy] to suffer in this name.**

When we come forth and begin to speak the truth, we
learn to walk in the Spirit and keep ourselves renewed. The
Spirit of God works in us and we go forth with the
commandment of God. When accusations come, take no
thought of it because if you suffer as a Christian, you should
not be ashamed but let God be glorified on His behalf.

Don't Get to Meddlin'

๑ ๑ ๑

We are then warned what not to do — murder, steal, be a
mischief maker or a meddler in other people's business. Not
many of us are murderers and thieves, but how many are guilty
of gossiping about others or meddling in their affairs? Our
tongues can be deadly weapons. The Word says we don't have a
right to do that. The only right we have is in Christ Jesus.

As you are learning to keep yourself renewed by
walking in the Spirit and knowing the way of the Spirit in
your life, do not be ashamed to stand up when someone is
trying to be a busybody. Simply tell them lovingly and
calmly that it is none of their business. Don't be rude but
explain to them that they are not operating in obedience to
God's Word. Too often, we neglect putting people in their
place by speaking the truth in love.

John 16:33 says,

**These things I have spoken unto you, that in
me ye might have peace. In the world ye shall have**

> tribulation: but be of good cheer; I have overcome
> the world.

Jesus went through all this tribulation victoriously. He is our perfect example, and He has given us His Word and the Holy Spirit. He says we are to be of good cheer because He has overcome, and we can too. You can stay in that overcoming position at all times by walking in the Spirit.

FILL YOURSELF WITH THE WORD

ട ട ട

There are so many Scriptures pertaining to tribulation and suffering. Most Christians don't want to even think about it, but in these days in which we live, we must fill ourselves with the Word so that we can endure to the end. First Thessalonians 3:4 AMP says,

> **For even when we were with you, [you know]**
> **we warned you plainly beforehand that we were to**
> **be pressed with difficulties *and* made to suffer**
> **affliction, just as to your own knowledge it has**
> **[since] happened.**

We have been warned. It is going to happen. But you can endure and through faith you can be victorious and remain victorious in *every* situation.

KNOW WHO YOU ARE

ട ട ട

The Word brings us encouragement in the face of such trials and affliction. We must know who we are IN CHRIST. First Peter 2:9-25 says,

But ye are a chosen generation, a royal priesthood, an holy nation, a peculiar people; that ye should shew forth the praises of him who hath called you out of darkness into his marvellous light: Which in time past were not a people, but are now the people of God: which had not obtained mercy, but now have obtained mercy.

Dearly beloved, I beseech you as strangers and pilgrims, abstain from fleshly lusts, which war against the soul; Having your conversation honest among the Gentiles: that, whereas they speak against you as evildoers, they may by your good works, which they shall behold, glorify God in the day of visitation. Submit yourselves to every ordinance of man for the Lord's sake: whether it be to the king, as supreme; Or unto governors, as unto them that are sent by him for the punishment of evildoers, and for the praise of them that do well.

For so is the will of God, that with well doing ye may put to silence the ignorance of foolish men: As free, and not using your liberty for a cloak of maliciousness, but as the servants of God. Honour all men. Love the brotherhood. Fear God. Honour the king.

Servants, be subject to your masters with all fear; not only to the good and gentle, but also to the froward. For this is thankworthy, if a man of conscience toward God endure grief, suffering wrongfully. For what glory is it, if, when ye be buffeted for your faults, ye shall take it patiently? but if, when ye do well, and suffer for it, ye take it patiently, that is acceptable with God. For even hereunto were ye called: because Christ also suffered for us, leaving us an example, that ye should follow his steps:

Who did no sin, neither was guile found in His mouth: Who when he was reviled, reviled not again; when he suffered, he threatened not; but committed himself to him that judgeth righteously: Who His own self bare our sins in his own body on the tree, that we, being dead to sins, should live unto right-eousness: by whose stripes ye were healed. For ye were as sheep going astray; but are now returned unto the Shepherd and Bishop of your souls.

Jesus suffered all of this. He walked as a servant of God. He was good not only to the gentle (kind, considerate and reasonable) but also to the froward (overbearing, unjust and crooked). We are not always good to the gentle *and* to the froward, are we?

JESUS OUR EXAMPLE

Jesus' suffering was an example, but there was a differ-ence between the suffering that He suffered on the cross as our substitute and the suffering He suffered on this earth for the Word's sake — for Truth. Through it all the Spirit of God was working His way in Him, keeping Him perfected so that He came through His life on this earth perfect.

He bore upon Himself *all* the sin, *all* the pain, *all* the disease that we had, as our substitute, that we might be free. So we don't have to suffer sickness, we don't have to suffer pain, and we don't have to suffer sin because He went to the cross for us. They were laid on Him. He was our substitute and suffered in our place. If we live according to the Word of God, the only sufferings we will suffer are opposition and persecution for the Word's sake or for the sake of the Truth because those that live godly lives in Christ Jesus shall suffer persecution.

I used to get accused of being too holy, of being "Miss Goodie Two Shoes." I would say to myself, "I just need to learn to be a little bit carnal," but in my mind I was already carnal enough. Those words were not the words of the Father. We need to discern what is being said to us. Is it a sidetrack to get us looking at other things or to get us feeling inadequate? I don't think any of us can be too holy. Most of the time, we are too carnal.

Get it down on the inside of you that, yes, trials and tribulations are going to come, but you have not been left destitute or hopeless. Jesus gave us an example, and it was perfected in Him. He has given to us all that He had — the Word and the Spirit — and that is all we need.

As I said before, God has His own way in working out His will in our lives. When we know what the Word of God says, then we will learn to discern these two things. We will learn to discern when it is simply an attack of the Devil, and we will learn when it is God leading us that way for a purpose. Smith Wigglesworth once said, "Great victories come out of great battles."

FIGHT FOR VICTORY

§ § §

How are you ever going to have a victory if you have never gone through a temptation, test or trial? You can't.

Even in sports like football and boxing, there is always a champion. There can't be champions without great battles. It has to be fought out. What we need to recognize is that our fight is not with the natural human man, but our fight is with the principalities and the powers of this earth.

> **For we wrestle not against flesh and blood, but against principalities, against powers, against the rulers of the darkness of this world, against spiritual wickedness in high places. Wherefore, take unto you the whole armour of God, that ye may be able to withstand in the evil day, and having done all, to stand.**
>
> **Ephesians 6:12**

We have within us what it takes to come against and defeat principalities and powers and remain victorious. We have the armour and the weapons we need to come against them. The trial of your faith is more precious than gold, and all of these are opportunities to grow and develop in the nature of God. There is always victory if you hold steady, maintain the Spirit and remain the same.

I don't think we really realize what it means when it says in Hebrews 13:8, **Jesus Christ the same yesterday, today, and for ever.** What that means is that He is the same as He has always been, and whatever opposition came against Him, He remained the same. He did what He has always done. He remained full of the Spirit and spoke the Word. What will cause you to remain the same is staying full of the Spirit and speaking the Word. You won't be up and down and in and out and wavering — you will *remain the same, not wavering.*

Did you know that your faith does not grow by feeding on the Word alone? Just like your body does not develop by only feeding it, you have to exercise it. You have to exercise your faith by putting your faith to work against the force of the enemy. When you understand that through these trials and testings, there is victory, then you will do what you know to do, staying full of the Holy Ghost and speaking the Word with boldness. Remember some of the hardest tests you go through are really God's way of leading you into a deeper place with Him — to draw you to Him so you really begin to seek Him.

We have been born again, we have become new creatures in Christ, and the Holy Spirit has come to live in us, to indwell us and to make His power real to us. But He can't do it if we don't let Him. So it is a matter of responding to Him and not to our own thinking, responding to His ways and not to our own ways.

BECOMING SPIRIT CONSCIOUS

§ § §

Sometimes in trusting God for physical healing, we are inclined to have faith for a minor affliction — a headache, stomach flu or a cold — but when something major comes, we begin to waver because we are too body-conscious instead of Spirit-conscious or Word-conscious. I'm sure you have heard this Scripture time and time again in Romans 4:19-20 talking about Abraham:

> **And being not weak in faith, he considered not**
> **his own body now dead, when he was about an**
> **hundred years old, neither yet the deadness of**

Sarah's womb: He staggered not at the promise of God through unbelief; but was strong in faith, giving glory to God.

Abraham considered not his own body. In other words, he saw the promise of God and not the greatness of the need. If we are not walking in the Spirit and do not know the way of the Spirit in our lives, we won't see the promise of God instead of the problem. Abraham believed God was able to perform any promise which He made to him. See, right here we can learn the way of the Spirit. When we pray and get worse instead of better, what are we to learn? We finally learn that divine healing does not depend on our physical state, but upon the quickening of the Holy Spirit. We have already read in Romans 8:11:

But if the Spirit of him that raised up Jesus from the dead dwell in you, he that raised up Christ from the dead shall also quicken your mortal bodies by his Spirit that dwelleth in you.

That same Spirit dwells in you. God is trying to bring us to the point where we are at the end of trusting in ourselves. We have a God Who can raise the dead. He is trying to get us to the point that our confidence and our trust is totally in Him, flowing His way, learning the way of His Spirit in our lives, coming into the freedom of the truth.

CHAPTER 12

Praying With Power

§ § §

We need to learn the way of the Holy Spirit in intercession, which is praying on behalf of others. The Scriptures tell us to pray the Word because the Word is truth, and the Word is what accomplishes things on the earth. In praying the truth through intercession, things do get done because we are speaking the desires of God. His Word is His truth and His desires.

When we have the Spirit of God on the inside of us, we can yield ourselves to the Holy Spirit knowing that we will pray the *perfect* prayer for each specific situation, and it will be accomplished. We can't do that within ourselves, but it is one of the ways the Spirit works in our lives not only for us but for others.

PRAYING FOR OTHERS

§ § §

When we intercede, we become one with the Holy Spirit, and people are birthed into the kingdom of God. They experience protection, healings and many other blessings which come from the Spirit of God operating in their lives.

These things happen in people's lives because the Holy Spirit makes intercession according to the will of God. Whether or not God lets us know what the actual things are that we are praying about, it doesn't really matter.

When you give of yourself and of your time for intercession, you will be blessed by becoming more aware that God is love. As you are praying you may see a person in your mind, and you can go to the Scriptures and begin to pray a specific Word over them because you had some knowledge of it. However, if you yield totally to the Holy Spirit, He can take you further in and accomplish it totally in the spirit realm so it will be manifested in the natural realm. Let the Holy Spirit help you pray because He knows how to pray the perfect prayer.

HAVE CONFIDENCE IN GOD

ଶ୍ର   ଶ୍ର   ଶ୍ର

When we learn the ways of the Spirit and yield ourselves to the Spirit, we have to have confidence in the Spirit of God Who is working through us in truth to accomplish things for His kingdom. When we have received the fullness of the Holy Spirit within us, we are endued with power from on high, and we will see people differently. We will be impressed to pray for others in a way we have never done before.

With that power added to our lives and prayer lives, others are benefited, but we also receive blessings. I already mentioned that it is the Holy Spirit working and doing His work within us Who brings the pureness and righteousness and the fruit to cause us to walk in godliness and God's perfect will every day. If we let the Holy Spirit do this work in us, we will be strong when temptation comes and not fail.

God works with different people differently. Don't try to compare yourself with others because you are unique and God's way with you will be unique. We need to learn the way of the Spirit in our own lives so that we can trace God in the circumstances of life that confront us. We will be victorious in those confrontations if we have learned the way God works by His Spirit within us.

THE HOLY SPIRIT WILL HELP US PRAY

Someone who is newly born again and is conscious of a need of his own or the need of another, may feel inadequate in knowing what words to use in praying for the need. The Holy Spirit, Who came to live inside him at the new birth, will help him pray.

> **Likewise the Spirit also helpeth our infirmities: for we know not what we should pray for as we ought: but the Spirit itself maketh intercession for us with groanings which cannot be uttered. And he that searcheth the hearts knoweth what is the mind of the Spirit, because he maketh intercession for the saints according to the will of God.**
>
> **Romans 8:26-27**

Romans 8:26 says, **Likewise the Spirit also helpeth our infirmities.** "Infirmities" can mean sickness or disease, but "infirmities" can also mean any hindrance. In the case of a new believer, the infirmity is simply not knowing how to pray as he ought. The Holy Spirit will help him. When the new believer feels inadequate in knowing how to pray for a need, a sigh or a groan is the best expression the prayer can produce. God will interrupt that groan of the Spirit and answer the prayer.

Once we are endued with power from on high and are filled with the Spirit, we have added power in prayer. We can pray with other tongues just as it says in Acts 2:4:

> **And they were all filled with the Holy Ghost, and began to speak with other tongues, as the Spirit gave them utterance.**

And as we saw in Romans 8:26, when we do not know how to pray anymore as we ought, the Holy Spirit will help us and groanings will come. God works in and through the groanings of the Spirit to get things accomplished.

REVELATION KNOWLEDGE THROUGH PRAYER

§ § §

When we pray in the Spirit, we begin to receive revelation. Sometimes the revelation we receive may be about our ministries or about things that God wants us to do. But just because God reveals something to us does not mean we are supposed to do it right then. Many times we want to jump in and get what God told us done tomorrow, or yesterday, when doing it immediately is not necessarily what God meant. If we get out of the timing or the season of God, we begin to do things our way rather than the Holy Spirit's way, and we get into trouble!

When God reveals something to us about situations in our church, He may simply be revealing something to us so that we can concentrate on it in prayer to get something done. Instead of jumping up and saying, "I've got a revelation from God. Do you know what He told me?" what we really need to do is pray and keep our mouths shut!

There are things, even in our ministries, that during prayer, God may tell us to do and not discuss, because it is not time to discuss them. The more we talk, the greater the possibility is that the Devil will get in and make a mess of things because he will try to stop anything that is of God. If we do, we allow the enemy to come in and tear up what God intended to do by speaking with our own mouths things we should not speak out yet because we have not learned to wait on the Spirit and know His way.

WHAT, HOW, WHY AND WHEN?

When God reveals things to us through intercessory prayer or through just praying in the Spirit for ourselves, we need to seek Him further about the revelation that He gives us to make sure we understand it clearly. We need to stop and say, "Okay God, you've given me this revelation. What do you want me to do with it?"

There are times when God speaks to you that you have a part to play in bringing it to pass, and there are other times that He is just letting you be aware of something He wants you to thank Him for and wait on Him to do. When God begins to give you revelation about your life or others, ask Him questions in these four areas: what, how, why and when.

So often, rather than seeking God and asking Him what He meant, then following what He tells us so that the Holy

Spirit can be working with us, we try to do something within ourselves. We say, "Well, this is what God said, and I'm going to do it." If we do not do something by and with the Spirit of God in His timing, it will be our own doing, and it will fail. We need to recognize the Spirit of God in these things and be able to discern whether they are or are not God.

Many times we know what, how and why but not when. Therefore, we move out too quickly and everything gets scrambled. Trying to unscramble the situation ourselves is like trying to unscramble scrambled eggs. Once they are scrambled, they are scrambled!

When we try to do things within ourselves and get into a mess, it puts us back. We not only have to catch up where we messed up, but we have to regain that knowledge we would have gained if we had stayed on course. It is difficult to get everything straightened out as it should be. But because of God's mercy, grace and truth, eventually we get ourselves back in line with the Spirit Who can unscramble everything. In prayer, we need to ask God for the timing of the season to keep us out of trouble!

REST IN GOD OR TAKE ACTION?

ṣ ṣ ṣ

There is a fine line in ministry and in our own lives between the times God wants us to do nothing but wait, rest in Him and simply let Him bring something to pass, and the times when God wants us to get up, push and play a part in bringing things to pass. We need to be able to discern the difference in our own spirits.

After we walk with God for a while and let Him work with us, we will be able to learn the way that the Spirit deals with us and will be able to discern the difference. We will learn to rest in Him so that we are able to clearly hear His voice and know whether to rest in Him in that particular situation or to take action. We will be able to discern what God wants us to do and when and how. We will learn how not to jump to conclusions.

WORKING THROUGH HARDSHIPS

ﾚ ﾚ ﾚ

So often we lose time and waste energy and go through many hardships that we would not have had to go through if we had just found out "when." There is a difference between you bringing hardships on yourself and God working through hardships to perfect some things through you and in you.

The Holy Ghost leads us according to where we are in spiritual development. Many times during the periods of waiting, even after God has told us the "when," God leads us through some wildernesses. He does this to get some of the ego or pride out of us so that when we begin to go forth with what He is telling us and mighty things begin to happen, we are humbled rather than caught up in pride over what is happening in *our* ministries.

WHAT WAS IT LIKE???

ﾚ ﾚ ﾚ

People come up to me all the time and say, "What was it like to grow up in the home of Kenneth Hagin?" To me, it was just like anybody else growing up in any other home. He is my daddy. It really wasn't so different because the truths that he has now, he didn't have when I was a baby and a little girl. He had to grow in the knowledge of the truth just like all of us do. Everything wasn't perfect all the time. After all, he isn't Jesus.

People have the idea because they see this great man of God that I must have lived in this outstanding home. Now it is not that it wasn't a good home because it was. It was full of love, and it was full of the Word of God and full of the Spirit of God. Even though he was still learning and growing, he always put God and the Word of God and the Spirit of God first, and we were taught that. But at the same time, we were a family, and we had hardships just like everybody else.

Because of the type of person I am, I don't see my life as being any different than others around me. But with all the attention given to my father, it would be very dangerous for me to allow myself to get puffed up in pride. There is no doubt that the priorities of setting God first, the solid biblical teaching, and the spiritual examples set in our home as I grew up have helped me avoid some pitfalls in life, and I am blessed.

Sometimes we fail to recognize when we think more highly of ourselves than we should. We must be careful when God begins to speak to us that pride and ego don't enter in. We must humble ourselves before the Lord and let Him work His way in us to get that pride out of us so we don't make mistakes. We must not get caught up in pride and say, "Look at me and look at my ministry and look what I have done."

The ministry is God's, not ours. We must take the time to learn the way of the Holy Spirit, letting ourselves develop spiritually so that we do not think and do things our own way, but instead we must follow the Spirit's way of thinking and doing. Then we must walk in His timing.

WE CAN ALWAYS LEARN MORE FROM THE HOLY SPIRIT

As we develop in the Spirit realm, we begin to realize how little we know about Him and His ways. When we think we know so much, we find out we know so little. Let me share with you how I learned a lesson from the Lord in this area.

I was speaking at a church conference, and I made this statement, "You know, I consider myself a novice in this." The Spirit of the Lord got on my case, but I have learned that the Spirit of the Lord is comforting even when he is correcting.

Doyle Tucker, the music leader, went over to the piano and said, "I have this song for you." He began to play a beautiful melody. I can't recall the exact words but the Spirit was saying I was no longer to call myself a novice. In my mind, I had thought, "God I don't know anything." But the song Doyle ministered showed me how from a little girl my heart was to follow God, and I had developed my prayer life because I loved God and wanted a relationship with Him. Because of that relationship from childhood, there were things in my spirit I didn't even realize were there, and they would come forth.

You see, the things you have in your spirit can't be comprehended by your mind, so you don't know they are there. They are there because you have a relationship with God, and you are being taught by Him, by His Spirit and by His Word. So we have to be careful how we speak things forth. There are some other areas in which I am a novice, but in this area God made it clear I was not to call myself a novice. I was blessed by Doyle's song from the Lord because I knew that in that one area I had grown.

We need to pray, "Lord, teach me what I don't know, show me what I don't see, and prepare me to receive what you have for me." When we pray this way, He will prepare us, but usually not in the way we think He will do it.

Of course, preparing ourselves in an area is easier on us than experiencing God doing it, but there are some things in the Spirit realm we will never get into if we do not let God stir us. We have to allow Him to stir us so that we can see things clearly regarding what He wants us to do or where He wants us to go. Too often in our natural minds, we look at our inabilities and think, "God wouldn't want me to do that!" He wants us to discern by His Spirit and to realize that *we can do it in His ability.*

We must always be open to learning more from the Holy Spirit because when we think we know so much, we become conscious of self, and if we are not careful, we get a self-righteous attitude. No matter what the Spirit of God is doing, we automatically say, "Yeah, I know that. You don't have to tell me." That is a lie, because not everybody knows everything the Spirit is doing all the time.

Most of the time, it is the women who do this, but some men fall into this, too. Women tend to be more susceptible to this way of thinking because, as a general rule, in our own human spirits, we are more sensitive than men. (God put in women a special sensitivity toward men to help wives support their husbands.) But we ladies need to learn the difference between what we are picking up in our own human spirits and what the Spirit of God is showing and telling us. Many times I can walk into a room and pick up on what is going on in people, in their spirits, but that does not mean it was the Holy Spirit telling me.

Just because our spirits are sensitive does not mean that we ladies are super-spiritual people and know everything in the Spirit. But often women take that attitude. I'm the type of person who sits and listens. I'm not a great conversationalist. I sit and listen and observe and watch. You learn a lot that way. I have seen women who think they are interpreting what the Spirit is going to do, then when the Spirit moves, their attitude is, "Well, I already knew that." They do not receive fully what God is doing because they are so "spiritual" they thought they already knew what would happen.

We need to be careful to know the difference between it being just us recognizing something in our own spirits and it being the Spirit of God making us aware of something. And remember that the Spirit always makes us aware of things for a purpose, not just so we can tell people that we hear from God.

Why did He let us know something? What was the purpose? We had better pray and find out. Can you see how neglectful we have been of learning the way of the Spirit and of learning how to follow the Spirit in our lives?

CAUTION! WARNING!

ᏍᎦ ᏍᎦ ᏍᎦ

In learning the way of the Spirit, be very careful when God by His Spirit begins to move and minister personally to people. Many people say, "I wish God would speak to me like that." I have found that when He comes forth with a supernatural manifestation that seems really great, the person had better be ready because there is a hard place ahead, and God is preparing him.

Unless you are ready for the growth that comes through that preparation, use wisdom and be careful what you say when the Spirit of the Lord begins to move through someone and there is personal prophecy. If you aren't ready to go through that hard time of preparation, instead of being desirous of that kind of move of God, just begin to rejoice and say, "Lord I just hope I don't need that kind of manifestation!"

Another caution, which seems to be prevalent in charismatic circles, is to not let "The Lord told me..." become a cliché. The things of God should not be clichés. Sometimes it seems like everybody you talk to is saying, "The Lord told me..." "The Lord told me..." They can't tell you anything without saying the Lord told them.

One of my closest friends got caught up in that, and finally one day I said, "Don't you know anything within yourself? Does God have to tell you everything, or do you feel so inadequate in your spiritual walk with Him that you have to appear spiritual by wanting people to know that God talks to you?" She looked at me rather surprised and said, "Thank you for saying that to me. I didn't even realize I was doing it."

It becomes a cliché. It is the "in" thing to say. When you keep going around constantly saying, "The Lord told me this and the Lord told me that," pretty soon the Lord isn't telling you anything because He wasn't telling you anything in the first place.

Do not take this lightly. Do you understand what I'm saying to you? Do you know what you do to your reputation because you have been saying all this time the Lord said this and the Lord said that? Eventually you begin to imagine, "Well God said this to me," and you open yourself up to familiar spirits. Then you are in real trouble.

Guard yourself and make sure you are not just saying something because you have heard somebody else say it. Make sure you are not getting caught up in clichés because it is the "in" thing to say. Because if you go around saying, "The Lord said," and the Lord hasn't said, when you begin to seek the Lord, He is not going to say anything to you because you have been out there as a false witness. You must come before Him and humble yourself and repent. Then, He will begin to speak to you.

Be cautious about saying, "The Lord told me," and be sure that He said it. Then seek His purpose about whether to share it or be still and look at how God works by His Spirit in your life to bring it about. Probably 90% of the time we need to keep quiet instead of talking about what God is saying to us or doing in our lives.

BE STRONG IN THE WORD AND THE SPIRIT

We must be strong in both the Word and the Spirit. We must know the Spirit of God because there are places He will lead us to and there are places that He will tell us we cannot go. Hearing correctly can mean life or death.

A lot of times we get the idea because there is not a lot happening that we missed God. We get our eyes on the circumstances and say, "Well, I must have missed God because only one person got saved." Did you ever think God might have led you that way for that one meeting to reach that one person? But in our minds, we have a week-long meeting, and if only one person got saved, we say, "That must not have been the will of God." Who said?

DON'T BE RULED BY THE SPECTACULAR

God will go to any length to reach one person. We get the idea that if it is not some great spectacular event, that is proof it wasn't God. Many times the supernatural things of God are not spectacular and most people don't even know they happened. But every day the supernatural power of God is working effectively in your life. Whether it is spectacular or not has nothing to do with it.

Other times, God uses the spectacular to keep us steady because it will make us aware that He is moving, and we aren't out there in left field. He is doing what He said He would do. We need to just be still so that we can see the difference and see how God is working.

In Acts 16, Paul was in prison because he cast a demon out of the servant woman who was possessed with the spirit of divination, and her masters were angry. Some people might have been saying, "He missed God or all that would not have happened." But Paul had had a vision and God had spoken to him. Even though he had been there many days and only one woman, Lydia, had been saved and one servant girl had had the devil cast out of her, he stood fast and did not waver.

When Paul and Silas got thrown in jail, they knew they were in God's plan, and they held steady because of the spectacular way in which God had moved with the vision that He gave to Paul. But you see, Paul didn't go around telling everyone "I had this vision". He just went and did what God said.

Paul and Silas didn't get discouraged because in the natural things looked dismal. They sat in prison praying and singing praises to God despite the fact their backs were bleeding and raw from the lashes they had received, and their feet were fastened in stocks. That was when God used the natural circumstances of an earthquake, which opened the prison doors, to do something supernatural — open the jailer's heart to salvation. That had been God's plan all along, and when it was fulfilled, Paul and Silas were set free.

We must not let the spectacular always rule us in discerning whether or not we are hearing God. God works in mysterious ways, sometimes with the obvious, but more often with the obscure. He just wants us to hear and obey, and by His Spirit He will empower us to do what He has called us to do.

This is serious business. We are in life–and–death situations every day. We must learn how to pray and follow the way of the Spirit in all things, doing what we know to do daily to develop the fullness of the Holy Spirit within us. If we don't do that or if we allow "self" to rule, a little bit of death will come each time we give our enemy, Satan, an open door for him to come in and start to steal, kill and destroy.

CHAPTER 13

Manifestations and Gifts of the Holy Spirit

ரூ ரூ ரூ

In chapter one we learned that the Holy Spirit comes to dwell *in* us when we are born again, but the fullness, or outpouring, of the Holy Spirit's power comes *upon* us. Being endued with power from on high, being filled with the Holy Spirit and being baptized with the Holy Spirit are all ways of stating that the infusion of the Holy Spirit brings power into our lives.

HOLINESS AND POWER

ரூ ரூ ரூ

We also have learned that the indwelling is to benefit the individual, and the fruit of the Holy Spirit is for *holiness*. We can see in Galatians 5:22-23 that the indwelling of the Holy Spirit is for bearing fruit: **But the fruit of the Spirit is love, joy, peace, longsuffering, gentleness, goodness, faith, Meekness, temperance: against such there is no law.**

The outpouring of the Holy Spirit is for *service*. Just as there are nine fruits of the Spirit, we can see in the passage below there are nine manifestations of the Holy Spirit. We can be holy without having power, and we can have power without being holy. God intended that we have both.

Now about spiritual gifts (the special endowments of supernatural energy), brethren, I do not want you to be misinformed. You know that when you were heathen, you were led off after idols that could not speak — habitually — as impulse directed *and* whenever the occasion might arise. Therefore I want you to understand that no one speaking under the power *and* influence of the (Holy) Spirit of God can [ever] say, Jesus be cursed! And no one can [really] say, Jesus is [my] Lord, except by *and* under the power *and* influence of the Holy Spirit.

Now there are distinctive varieties *and* distributions of endowments [gifts, extraordinary powers distinguishing certain Christians, due to the power of divine grace operating in their souls by the Holy Spirit] and they vary, but the (Holy) Spirit remains the same. And there are distinctive varieties of service *and* ministration, but it is the same Lord [Who is served]. And there are distinctive varieties of operation — of working to accomplish things — but it is the same God Who inspires *and* energizes them all in all. But to each one is given the manifestation of the (Holy) Spirit — that is, the evidence, the spiritual illumination of the Spirit — for good and profit.

To one is given in *and* through the (Holy) Spirit [the power to speak] a message of wisdom, and to another [the power to express] a word of knowledge *and* understanding according to the same (Holy) Spirit; To another (wonder-working) faith by the same (Holy) Spirit, to another the extraordinary powers of healing by the one Spirit; To another the working of miracles, to another prophetic insight — the gift of interpreting the divine will and purpose; to another the ability to discern *and* distinguish between [the utterances of true] spirits [and false ones], to another various kinds of [unknown] tongues, to another the ability to interpret [such] tongues.

All these [achievements and abilities] are inspired *and* brought to pass by one and the same (Holy) Spirit, Who apportions to each person individually [exactly] as He chooses.

1 Corinthians 12:1-11 AMP

When we learn to walk in the Spirit and learn the way of the Spirit, these manifestations will begin to operate in our lives. However, they are not manifested for our individual benefit, or even for the Church, but for our everyday walk in the world because the manifestations are for us to bless others.

There are nine manifestations: (1) the word of wisdom, (2) the word of knowledge, (3) special faith, (4) gifts of healings, (5) working of miracles, (6) prophecy, (7) discerning of spirits, (8) divers kinds of tongues, and (9) interpretation of tongues. All of these manifestations are by the same Spirit. The manifestation of the Spirit is for every man.

Read 1 Corinthians 12 in the Amplified Bible, but for this study, I am going back to the King James Version. First

Corinthians 12:1 states: **Now concerning spiritual gifts, brethren, I would not have you ignorant.** The meaning of the original Greek is "now concerning things pertaining to and of the Holy Ghost, I would not have you ignorant."[1] Now the whole twelfth chapter of 1 Corinthians makes sense: it is discussing the ministry gifts that are pertaining to and of the Holy Spirit and the Body of Christ that is pertaining to and of the Holy Spirit. The general subject of the chapter is not spiritual gifts, and the specific subject is not the gifts of the Spirit.

Look again at verse 4: **Now there are diversities of gifts, but the same Spirit.** All of these nine manifestations are not *necessarily* gifts of the Spirit. They are simply ways in which the Holy Spirit manifests Himself. However, some of them are gifts because the verse says there are diversities of gifts. Some are administrations and some are operations. (vv. 5, 6.)

Generally speaking, all of these manifestations of the Spirit are gifts because they have been given, but *specifically* speaking, they are not all gifts.

The words "gift" or "gifts" are translated from different words in the Greek language. In the Greek, the manner of giving and the nature of the gift determined what word should be used to express the meaning. Greek words for "gift" or "gifts" and their definitions are discussed below. In this book, we are primarily concerned with definitions "3," *merismos,* and "4," *charisma,* which is the word for "gifts" in 1 Corinthians 12:1: **Now concerning spiritual gifts, brethren, I would not have you ignorant.**

1. *Dorea* means gratuity.[2] One reference book gives a meaning of this word as "giving to a pauper." This Greek word is mentioned in the Scriptures on salvation and also on the gift of the Holy Spirit. In either case, whether salvation or the receiving of the Holy Spirit, the recipient is a poor man who is utterly without spiritual life or power. Unless God in His great mercy gives these to him, he will always be that way.

John 4:10 states:

> **Jesus answered and said unto her, If thou knewest the *gift of God*, and who it is that saith to thee, Give me to drink; thou wouldest have asked of him, and he would have given thee living water** [Gift, gratuity, new birth.]

Acts 2:38 states:

> **Then Peter said unto them, Repent, and be baptized every one of you in the name of Jesus Christ for the remission of sins, and ye shall receive *the gift of the Holy Ghost*.** [Gift, gratuity, Holy Spirit. We obtain both through faith and by the merits of the shed blood of the Lord Jesus Christ. Because we are paupers or poor men, through Jesus Christ God gives us these gifts so we can become rich and strong and operate in all that He has.]

2. *Doron* means a present or an offering, or sacrifice.[3]

Ephesians 2:8 states:

> **For by grace are ye saved through faith; and that not of yourselves: *it is the gift of God*.** [A gift of

God — in other words, the faith that we were saved by was not of ourselves; it was a gift of God.]

3. *Merismos* means a separation or distribution: dividing asunder, gift.[4]

Hebrews 2:1-4 states:

> **Therefore we ought to give the more earnest heed to the things which we have heard, lest at any time we should let them slip. For if the word spoken by angels was stedfast, and every transgression and disobedience received a just recompence of reward; How shall we escape, if we neglect so great salvation; which at the first began to be spoken by the Lord, and was confirmed unto us by them that heard him; God also bearing them witness, both with signs and wonders, and with divers miracles, and *gifts of the Holy Ghost,* according to his own will?**

This speaks of distributions of the Holy Spirit that compare Christ and His Church. So, "distributions" would be measures of the Holy Spirit. For example, there are different measures in the offices of the anointing. Not everyone has the same anointing. They are different as the Holy Spirit distributes them.

John 3:34 states:

> **For he whom God hath sent speaketh the words of God: for God giveth not the Spirit by *measure* unto him.** (Measures, distributions.)

Ephesians 4:1-7 states:

> I therefore, the prisoner of the Lord, beseech you that ye walk worthy of the vocation wherewith ye are called, With all lowliness and meekness, with longsuffering, forbearing one another in love; Endeavouring to keep the unity of the Spirit in the bond of peace.
>
> There is one body, and one Spirit, even as ye are called in one hope of your calling; One Lord, one faith, one baptism, One God and Father of all, who is above all, and through all, and in you all. But unto every one of us is given grace according to the *measure* of the gift of Christ.

Measure, distribution, implies that with us being the Body and Jesus the Head, the Body has the same measure that Jesus has, but as individual members we do not have the same measure.

4. *Charisma* means an endowment or miraculous faculty.[5] The word is used for the gift of prophecy.

Romans 12:6-8 states:

> Having then *gifts* differing according to the grace that is given to us, whether prophecy, let us prophesy according to the proportion of faith; Or ministry, let us wait on our ministering: or he that teacheth, on teaching; Or he that exhorteth, on exhortation: he that giveth, let him do it with simplicity; he that ruleth, with diligence; he that sheweth mercy, with cheerfulness.

This "charisma" is a gift, and it is talking about endowment of a miraculous faculty. We have these gifts differing according to the grace or measure that has been given to us. We prophesy according to the portion of another. In other words, we prophesy according to what will match up with someone else because we don't all have the same measure. I may prophesy in part or in the gifts and measure I have, and somebody else may prophesy in the measure and gift he has because we all don't have the full measure individually.

It is the same in teaching or in exhortation. It is an endowment from God by His Spirit, and therefore, we speak by the Spirit of God to those that are listening.

First Peter 4:10-11 states:

> **As every man hath received the *gift*, even so minister the same one to another, as good stewards of the manifold grace of God. If any man speak, let him speak as the oracles of God; if any man minister, let him do it as of the ability which God giveth: that God in all things may be glorified through Jesus Christ, to whom be praise and dominion for ever and ever. Amen.**

We must be good stewards of the grace or measure given to us by the Spirit. Sometimes we try to go past the grace God has given us because we have seen someone else operate in a different measure, but we have to stay within the limit of grace God has given to us individually. Our grace matched with someone else's grace, and then matched with someone else's grace, etc., will eventually make the Body of Christ a whole, full measure.

Acts 2:14-18 refers to prophesy.

> But Peter, standing up with the eleven, lifted
> up his voice, and said unto them, Ye men of
> Judaea, and all ye that dwell at Jerusalem, be this
> known unto you, and hearken to my words: For
> these are not drunken, as ye suppose, seeing it is
> but the third hour of the day. But this is that which
> was spoken by the prophet Joel;
>
> And it shall come to pass in the last days, saith
> God, I will pour out of my Spirit upon all flesh:
> and your sons and your daughters shall *prophesy,*
> and your young men shall see visions, and your
> old men shall dream dreams: And on my servants
> and on my handmaidens I will pour out in those
> days of my Spirit; and they shall *prophesy.*

Tongues and interpretation of tongues are simply prophecy
in its varied forms. (*Prophecy* means inspired utterance."[6])

Prophecy, as we are speaking about here, is in a known
tongue, our own language. Divers kinds of tongues is
inspired utterance in an unknown language (unknown to
us). Interpretation of tongues is inspired utterance by the
Holy Spirit giving forth the meaning of that which was
spoken. It is a divine illumination or revelation (not translation) by the Holy Spirit that explains what the Spirit said.
All of it is inspired utterance and, in the general sense,
prophecy. (Specifically speaking, tongues with interpretation is equivalent to prophecy.)

The Greek for the word "gifts" in 1 Corinthians 12:4
is *charisma.*

> Now there are diversities of *gifts,* but the same
> Spirit. [There are distributions of endowments or

miraculous faculty. Verse 9 refers to the gifts of healing by the same Spirit — endowments.]

The Greek word for "gifts" in Romans 11:29 is *charisma*.

For *the gifts* and calling of God are without repentance.

God's gifts — endowment or miraculous faculty — are without repentance. This verse leads us to believe that those things which can be properly called "gifts" are given outright and are to be used as we depend upon God to confirm His Word with signs following. (Mark 16:20 tells us, **And they went forth, and preached every where, the Lord working with them, and confirming the word with signs following.**)

The Bible tells us to give the gospel to the world. Mark 16:15 says, **Go ye into all the world, and preach the gospel to every creature.** God has *endowed* His Church with gifts proclaimed in word and in deed.

Verily, verily, I say unto you, He that believeth on me, the works that I do shall he do also; and greater works than these shall he do; because I go unto my Father.

John 14:12

And he said unto them, Go ye into all the world, and preach the gospel to every creature. He that believeth and is baptized shall be saved; but he that believeth not shall be damned. And these signs shall follow them that believe; In my name shall they cast out devils; they shall speak with new tongues; They shall take up serpents; and if they

drink any deadly thing, it shall not hurt them; they
shall lay hands on the sick, and they shall recover.

Mark 16:15-18

In this dispensation given to the Church is a threefold
manifestation of the prophetic office — speaking with
tongues, interpretation of tongues and prophecy. For physical
deliverance there are gifts of healings. Therefore, *specifically*
speaking, these four are called "gifts." "Speaking with tongues"
in the Scriptures is used in various ways, but in essence it is
one and the same. In purpose and use, it is varied.

Speaking with tongues manifests when born again
believers are baptized with or filled with the Holy Ghost.
This is a physical evidence.

> **And they were all filled with the Holy Ghost,
> and began to speak with other tongues, as the
> Spirit gave them utterance.**
>
> *Acts 2:4*

Ten years later:

> **While Peter yet spake these words, the Holy
> Ghost fell on all them which heard the word. For they
> heard them speak with tongues, and magnify God.**
>
> *Acts 10:44,46*

Twenty years later:

> **And when Paul had laid his hands upon them,
> the Holy Ghost came on them; and they spake with
> tongues, and prophesied.**
>
> *Acts 19:6*

195

Speaking with other tongues is used in addressing God in prayer, in worship and in song.

For he that speaketh in an unknown tongue speaketh not unto men, but unto God; for no man understandeth him; howbeit in the spirit he speaketh mysteries. [One translation calls these mysteries, "divine secrets." I like that. Tongues is a supernatural means of communication with the Father God.]

1 Corinthians 14:2

But ye, beloved, building up yourselves on your most holy faith, praying in the Holy Ghost. [Tongues edify and build us up spiritually. Praying in tongues is a spiritual exercise. Your spirit is in direct contact with God Who is a Spirit.]

Jude 20

For if I pray in an unknown tongue, my spirit prayeth, but my understanding is unfruitful. [God has devised a means whereby our spirits apart from our understanding may pray.]

1 Corinthians 14:14

A question I am often asked is, "How can I tell the difference between praying in the Spirit and speaking in tongues?" My answer is that they are the same thing.

THE IMPORTANCE OF INTERPRETATION

੮ ੮ ੮

The next question that immediately follows is, "But when someone is speaking in tongues, doesn't there have to be an interpretation? When I am praying in the Spirit, I'm not looking for an interpretation." My answer to that is, "You should be!" When you are praying in the Spirit to edify and build yourself up every day, you are praying in tongues. Even though your spirit knows what you are praying, you need to interpret it so that it not only affects your spirit but also your soul and your mind.

You just have to start where you are and allow your faith to be built up. As you pray in tongues more and more, your faith should build up to the point that when you get quiet, you will receive an interpretation of your worship and praise unto God and that tongue. This is how your soul and your mind will be edified along with your spirit.

We should be doing this every day because it is part of our growth. It is part of allowing the Spirit of God within us to grow us up and mature us privately so that when we come to a meeting, Colossians 3:16 will be manifested.

Let the word of Christ dwell in you richly in all wisdom; teaching and admonishing one another in psalms and hymns and spiritual songs, singing with grace in your hearts to the Lord.

We don't have to stay at one level. We can get to the point where our faith rises because we know that we know the voice of the Spirit. We have worshipped with Him enough that we know His voice. When this happens, we no longer have to pray, speak or sing in tongues and interpret. We can just go out and prophesy. It comes out in English or our own language.

Speaking with other tongues is also used in addressing the Church. It edifies, builds up and makes those who hear it aware of the presence of God.

> How is it then, brethren? when ye come
> together, every one of you hath a psalm, hath a
> doctrine, hath a tongue, hath a revelation, hath an
> interpretation. Let all things be done unto
> edifying. If any man speak in an unknown tongue,
> let it be by two, or at the most by three, and that
> by course; and let one interpret.
>
> **1 Corinthians 14:26-27**

Interpretation, like tongues, is for *all* people. In a service
and in public when someone speaks forth a message in
tongues, there should be an interpretation because there are
those there who are not spiritually mature and don't understand what is going on. Therefore, there needs to be an
interpretation for edification and understanding.

I know you are thinking, "Well, what about the times
when someone speaks forth in tongues and no interpretation comes?" There are times when someone may speak
out in tongues and no interpretation comes forth simply
because the person got carried away and excited in the
emotion of praying and blurted out what they were praying.
We need to be spiritually discerning to understand this can
happen when a group of people are worshipping God.

There is a difference between when someone is praying
in the Spirit or worshipping God and when God, by His
Spirit, is speaking forth a message in tongues for the Body.
Interpretation is important, but God sometimes surprises us
with how it is accomplished.

In our ministry, Buddy and I are used together in the
ministry of tongues and interpretation, which is equivalent
to prophecy. At a service one day, I was sitting on the very

first row in the balcony, and everybody was standing. It was right at the end of a powerful time of praise and worship, and there was a quiet time. I felt the Spirit of God moving within me, and I knew I was to speak forth in tongues. So I began to speak it forth. Since Buddy wasn't there that day, I expected someone from the platform to come forth with the interpretation, but it didn't happen. When I sat down, the Devil beat me over the head whispering in my ear, "You know you did that. That wasn't God. There wasn't an interpretation. You caused confusion, blah, blah, blah."

After the service, I found out the pastor didn't even hear it, so he couldn't interpret. Then a lady and a young man came up to me, and she said, "I want to introduce you to...." (I don't remember what his name was now.) She said, "He is from Lebanon. When you spoke forth in that tongue, you were standing in the first row in the balcony, and we were right down below you. He heard every word you said in his language. As a result, he received the Lord Jesus Christ!"

There is a uniqueness within itself of how the interpretation may take place. Tongues are for the edifying and building up of the believer, but they can also affect the unbeliever by getting their attention. The young man at the service I just told you about recognized that he was in the presence of God and that it was God speaking to his heart.

Man has more knowledge of spiritual things than we give him credit for. Unbelievers are very much aware of spiritual warfare going on within them. Just as you are aware of the spiritual warfare than goes on inside of you when the Devil is trying to steal the Truth from you, it is the same for the unbeliever. There comes that time when the Holy Spirit begins to draw him out of the darkness of Satan's kingdom into the kingdom of light. When this is happening unbelievers know something spiritual is going on, but not in the way we do because they don't have a knowledge or understanding of the Word.

WALKING BY FAITH NOT BY SIGHT

The Holy Spirit leads and guides us on the inside but He doesn't tell us everything. If He did, we wouldn't be walking in faith. We would be walking by sight. If we are going to please God, we must walk by faith and totally trust in Him, walking in that which we know and trusting Him with what we don't know. When we truly know Him, we can trust Him to perform in our lives what will be good.

We have to depend on the Holy Spirit and understand He will not do the same thing the same way every time. He will act according to the people that are present, according to their maturity level, according to their level of belief or unbelief, and many other factors. His ways are not our ways. When we get to the point that we think we know every-thing, that is when we are in trouble.

INTERPRETING THE MOVE OF THE SPIRIT

When the Scripture speaks about there being an inter-preter of the service, it doesn't mean one that interprets all the tongues. It means one that can interpret the move of the Holy Spirit in that service. Usually the pastor is able to do this.

That is why you must be very careful when someone speaks forth in tongues, and there doesn't seem to be an interpretation. Don't condemn or judge that person. Because if you are able to interpret that service by the Spirit, you will know if it is affecting someone.

Just praise God for what He is doing. If you are in tune with what is going on, you don't need a sign or an exact interpretation because you know by the Spirit someone is being ministered to. Unless you know for a fact someone is not speaking a word from God, you must be cautious about saying to someone, "You are out of order. Be quiet."

After a word is given in tongues, a time of quiet or stillness may occur before the interpretation comes. I have been in services when someone started speaking in tongues, and the Lord would give me the interpretation, but I was somewhat nervous about getting up to give it. A little while later, someone else stood up and came forth with the same interpretation I had gotten.

We need to get past the fear of man. When you are in tune with the Spirit and when God is moving, you may not know it word for word, but don't be afraid to speak it out. You will know what He is saying because you have His Spirit inside of you, and you will know in your spirit if you are supposed to give the interpretation. All interpretation is as the Spirit wills.

TUNING IN TO THE SPIRIT

๑ ๑ ๑

A lot of times we don't tune ourselves in to the Spirit because we expect the pastor or someone else to do it. Don't be afraid to exercise your gifts. Be a doer of the Word. It is the only way you will grow and mature. The Holy Spirit is our helper. He will help us by His Spirit when we are praying to God so we can have knowledge of what we are saying to Him. And at the same time, when someone else speaks forth in tongues, by His Spirit within us, we have the power to speak forth what God is saying to us and have understanding of it.

> **Wherefore let him that speaketh in an unknown tongue pray that he may interpret.**
>
> **1 Corinthians 14:13**

Prophecy is also for every believer.

> **For ye may all prophesy one by one, that all may learn, and all may be comforted.**
>
> **1 Corinthians 14:31**

Every believer can operate in simple prophecy. We are talking here about a gift of the Spirit that operates in all believers, not the function of a prophet.

Tongues, interpretation of tongues and prophecy are gifts which belong to all of us. They are so important that almost the entire fourteenth chapter of 1 Corinthians discusses how to use them.

These other manifestations of the Spirit which are the word of wisdom, the word of knowledge, discerning of spirits, special faith, working of miracles, are hardly mentioned, or Paul doesn't go into detailed instructions on how they operate in this chapter.

PAUL'S INSTRUCTIONS

⑤ ⑤ ⑤

Paul gave us all these instructions for speaking in tongues and interpretation of tongues and for prophecy because these are gifts that are given to the believer. You do it, and you operate in it to mature yourself *and* to speak forth what God has said and bless others. What good would it do for us to go around speaking in tongues all of the time if we never knew what we were saying to God or what God was saying to us? There are times when it is not important for us to know, but there are other times when it is very important. It can even be the difference between life and death. So we have to allow those gifts to operate in us to mature us to higher spiritual levels.

We need to rightly divide all this so we understand how we are walking in it and how it is to be operative in our lives. Speaking in tongues is used in a lot of different ways in the Word of God. It is used when we are filled with the Holy Spirit. It is used when we are speaking to God in worship, in prayer, in song, as a sign for the unbeliever.

BE SPIRIT-CONSCIOUS

⑤ ⑤ ⑤

In getting people free to let their spirit reign in their life, we have emphasized the freedom, but what happens when we become flesh and soulish-conscious rather than Spirit-conscious. We see this occur in praise and worship. We know we are to worship God in Spirit, but much of our worship is fleshly and soulish. The reason there is not a lot of spiritual demonstration when we worship God is because

it is not of the Spirit. We think we are following the way of
the Spirit, but in our so-called freedom, we are operating
out of our soulish, fleshly realm. Being Spirit-conscious is
the only way we can continue to follow the way of the Spirit
in our services as well as in our lives.

AS THE SPIRIT WILLS

The way to know what is the secret of the mystery
coming from God is to interpret it by the Spirit. Sometimes
that mystery is concerning the Church, and sometimes it is
concerning our own lives or the call of God on our lives. All
interpretation is as the Spirit wills. The Spirit desires for you
to grow, and when you call on Him, then you always have
that capacity within you to be able to interpret.

We can pray in tongues to build ourselves up anytime
because the Holy Spirit lives within us, and we have our
own prayer language that we get when we are filled with the
Holy Spirit. Sometimes we confuse our own tongue, or
prayer language, that we have when we receive the infilling
of the Holy Spirit with a tongue given by the Holy Spirit for
a specific purpose.

Have you ever been praying along in tongues and
building yourself up and worshipping God in the Spirit,
and, all of a sudden, it changes? What happened is that you
changed over from your own prayer language to the
language of the Spirit because God is beginning to use you
by His Spirit to affect something or someone such as in a
prayer of intercession. That is why the Scripture says there

are diversities of tongues. It is not all the same language or the same tongue.

If you listen to yourself, when you are just praying in the Spirit in your own language that you were given when you were filled with the Spirit, many times the words sound the same and have the same flow. When the Spirit moves you into another language, you can hear the difference in the sounds and feel the difference in the flow. You have connected with the Holy Spirit, and through divers kinds of tongues, you are speaking forth the will of the Father God for you as a whole or for an individual. Such tongues and interpretation is equivalent to prophecy.

If you have seen Buddy and I minister, I may prophesy or he may prophesy and that is for a purpose. Other times, I may give a tongue, and he may interpret. Each is for a purpose, because it is as the Spirit wills, and He knows how to direct that service so that it affects everybody that is there. Sometimes God may speak and say a certain thing is to happen. Our first inclination is to tell somebody. However, God is making you aware that you are in tune with the Spirit, and He may be saying to just sit back and watch Him do it. Or, He may be telling you to intercede for a time about it. This is part of learning the way of the Spirit.

Everything that is involved in the Spirit realm has to do with learning the way of the Holy Spirit as He is the one Who will help you get the job done. Since there is a mystery or unknown to the future, we must pray those things out or interpret our prayers by the Spirit of God. That way, He helps us to learn about our lives in God, flowing with His Spirit, and following in the fullness of it.

We have stopped God and the flow of the Spirit by confining these gifts to one use and one purpose. There is more to tongues than just being filled and speaking with tongues. That is good, and it has a purpose, but there are more purposes and uses for it. As the Spirit begins to move, if we are not careful, we are so blessed with the ecstasy of it, we fail to get what the Holy Spirit is endeavoring to give us because He not only teaches by precept but by example.

COMPLETE NINE-FOLD MANIFESTATION

The baptism with the Holy Spirit, taught in Acts 2:1-4, is the one and only way in which we are given the *complete* nine-fold manifestation of the Holy Spirit.

And when the day of Pentecost was fully come, they were all with one accord in one place. And suddenly there came a sound from heaven as of a rushing mighty wind, and it filled all the house where they were sitting. And there appeared unto them cloven tongues like as of fire, and it sat upon each of them. And they were all filled with the Holy Ghost, and began to speak with other tongues, as the Spirit gave them utterance.

Acts 2:1-4

So again what we are saying is that the infilling of the Holy Spirit is the door into the fullness of walking in the manifestations of the Spirit.

There are different gifts, differences of administration and differences or diversities of operations. And all are manifestations of the Spirit or the way the Spirit works. Four are gifts that belong to all of us — tongues, interpretation of tongues, prophecy and gifts of healing. The others — word of wisdom, word of knowledge, special faith, working of miracles, discerning of spirits — may be manifested to us or they may not. But you have the capacity for them because you have the Holy Spirit within you. Sometimes it is according to the office to which we are called. All of this is for a purpose in our lives as well as for the Church as a whole.

DO IT YOURSELF!

🕉 🕉 🕉

You need to pray in the Spirit and get direction for yourself and walk it out in victory. This is learning the way of the Spirit. Too often we want someone else to pray for us and get the answer for us.

James 5:13-15 AMP says:

> **Is anyone among you afflicted — ill-treated, suffering evil? He should pray. Is anyone glad at heart? He should sing praises [to God]. Is any one among you sick? He should call in the church elders — the spiritual guides. And they should pray over him, anointing him with oil in the Lord's name. And the prayer [that is] of faith will save him who is sick, and the Lord will restore him; and if he has committed sins, he will be forgiven.**

So what was he saying in verse 13 when he said, **Is anyone among you afflicted?** It means that if you are in trials and temptations and testings, *you* are to pray and get direction for yourself by the Spirit of God. In the King James it goes on to say, **Is any merry?** Does it say to get someone to do your singing for you? No, and we wouldn't think of that would we? How many times have you gone up to someone and said, "Will you sing for me?" Can you count how many times you have asked someone else to pray for you? What does that tell you? When you are going through those trials, temptations and testings, when you are afflicted, *you* pray. *You* get the mind of God and the direction of God. And if you are merry, then *you* sing. That is how you learn the way of the Spirit.

You are responsible for you. That is the reason you need to learn the way of the Spirit. That is the reason you need to have understanding of how the Spirit of God works. That is the reason you need to understand the gifts of the Spirit and the operations of the Spirit and the demonstrations of the Spirit. Hopefully then, you can properly bring understanding, not only to your life and situations, but to others as the Spirit wills.

MORE TIME AT THE ALTAR

§ § §

I believe that in our churches today more pastors need to call everybody down front to pray and spend time with God around the altar of God with people who are trained to pray. If you don't know exactly how to pray for yourself, you can get someone to help you and teach you. Then you can pray for your afflictions by the Spirit of God.

In James 5:14 it says, **Is anyone among you sick? He should call in the church elders.** Actually, the literal Greek means if you are beyond doing anything for yourself, then call for the elders of the church. But see, we want to call immediately for the elders. We should be asking, "Am I beyond the point where I can help myself by the Spirit of God and the Word of God?" If so, then it is time to call for the elders. We all get to that point sometimes, and there is nothing wrong with that.

We just need to understand what it means and what we need to do to be walking in the Spirit, learning the way of the Spirit and experiencing the fullness of it. We are not to be leaning on somebody else. We are to be leaning on God.

Administrations of the Spirit

ฬ ฬ ฬ

There are administrations of the Spirit which are the word of knowledge, the word of wisdom and the discerning of spirits. These help to give people insight into their situations in order to bring about godly results. A word of knowledge is not something that you conjure up from your own spirit. It is something that is spoken to you by the Spirit of God as the Spirit wills. You can't make it happen. If you get a word of knowledge, then God will give you directions regarding what you are supposed to do with it. It is between you and God. But because you know the Spirit and because you know that your life is controlled by the Spirit, then you know that you have heard the Spirit.

When you speak forth that word of knowledge by the Spirit of God, then you have to let it lie there if nobody responds. That doesn't mean that you were wrong or that you're bad or evil, nor does it mean the person that didn't respond is bad or evil. You aren't responsible for how someone else does or doesn't respond to a word of knowledge. People are really funny about things.

Some people can stand there knowing all the time it is for them, but they just don't want to acknowledge it in front of anyone else. After the service, they come and say, "You know, that was me. Will you pray for me?" I say, "No." When they ask, "Why?" I explain it is because the anointing is not there now; the flow of the Holy Spirit has left. Now I can pray for them as a believer, but there won't be that same anointing that came as the Spirit wills to relieve that person of their situation at that moment at that time. It is nothing I do within myself and nothing they do within themselves. When they respond to that word of knowledge, the Spirit of God will do it in them.

DIVERSITY OF OPERATIONS

§ § §

Then we have the diversity of operations, which are special faith and working of miracles. A good testimony guided by the Holy Spirit is prophecy. Why is that? Because you are under the inspiration of the Holy Spirit and you are giving forth a testimony of what God has done. Guided by the Holy Spirit, you are speaking forth a truth, what God wills at that time, and it will help somebody. It is for a purpose to bring somebody into an area of understanding of whatever God is working in him at that time. Therefore, you can be used in this way.

To predict the future is *not* the simple gift of prophecy. To prophesy is to speak unto men for edification, exhortation and comfort. There is a difference in the ministry of the prophet and prophesying. You may all prophesy, but not all are prophets. And that is where confusion comes in. A lot of people think because they prophesy that they must be a prophet, but that is not true.

What are gifts of healings? They are a supernatural manifestation of healing through one individual to another. Jesus was used in the gifts of healings. This gift is for physical healing. Not everyone operates in the same gifts of healings. Mark 16:17 says, **And these signs shall follow them that believe.** What was Jesus talking about? He was talking about healing with the exception of speaking with new tongues.

In other words, you will have these gifts of healings operating. Healing will come forth by the Spirit of God through you to another, but the new tongue comes from praying. By praying, we begin to operate in the Spirit in tongues, allowing our Spirit to join with the Holy Spirit to pray the perfect prayer.

People came to Jesus to be healed of diseases and of unclean spirits, and they were healed. Many times we call it casting out demons, but it is gifts of healings in operation. Jesus did these works, and we are to do them also. The Lord Jesus, the Head of the Church, administers through the Body for us to work and act supernaturally and carry out His will.

When people come to be healed, it involves a variety of diseases, unclean spirits and sicknesses. God may direct you to call the devil out, but many times through the gifts of healings, they just come out. You don't have to work forever to cast out that devil. When you operate through that healing gift that has been given to you by the Holy Spirit and you speak forth what the Spirit of God tells you to speak in the name of Jesus, healing comes, whether it is in disease or sickness or unclean spirits.

SPEAK THE WORD!

We put too much emphasis on the Devil and his power and what he can do. My Bible says, "Speak the Word." Speaking the Word by the Spirit of God brings freedom instantly. We operate so much in the soulish realm that we have to let the indwelling presence of the Spirit of God work healing in our soul and in our emotions. When we allow the Word of God by the indwelling presence of the Spirit of God to bring understanding to our soulish realm, we begin to mature in our soulish realm so that we can understand what is going on and yield ourselves to the Holy Spirit instead of the flesh and the soul.

The word of wisdom is a supernatural manifestation concerning His plan, purpose and will. The word of knowledge is a supernatural manifestation concerning facts in the mind of God because God knows everything. So the Holy Spirit can give you a word of wisdom about someone concerning God's plan or purpose or will in their life, and then, through the word of knowledge, He can give you direction so that you can know what to do about that word of wisdom. Jesus has to work through the Body of a Church. So just as our head can't do anything without our body, we, the Body, must to learn to listen to the Head, Jesus, and do His work by the Holy Spirit.

HEALING SPECIALTIES

𝔰 𝔰 𝔰

As I said already, in gifts of healings there are different areas involved, such as disease, unclean spirits and sickness. There is a difference in just being sick and having a disease. Different ministries operate in different areas. They have a different specialty. My father is used a lot in healing people that have knots or growths or hernias. It works every time. Why is that? That is the gifts of healings that God has given to him by the Spirit of God to operate in the Body of Christ.

However, he has laid hands on people in faith and the anointing has come, and other gifts of healings have been made manifest through him also. So we should not limit the Spirit of God. Even though there may be one area of gifts of healings in which you are used quite often, keep yourself tuned with the Spirit of God and in line with the Spirit of God, and He will use you in other gifts as well.

Exercise the gifts in which you operate. Acts 8:5-7 says,

> **Then Philip went down to the city of Samaria, and preached Christ unto them. And the people with one accord gave heed unto those things which Philip spake, hearing and seeing the miracles which he did. For unclean spirits, crying with loud voice, came out of many that were possessed with them: and many taken with palsies, and that were lame, were healed.**

Philip did these things. It says, **seeing the miracles which he did**. It wasn't within himself, but it was by the Spirit of God that he did it. Also notice that the healings were confined to certain areas: palsy, lameness and unclean spirits. In other words, Philip's endowments were in these areas. We are not to limit God, but often one gift or gifts of healing primarily operates in and through a person in their ministry.

A lot of times, the same type of healings can be accomplished through the gift of faith or special faith. Smith Wigglesworth said this, "When you have special faith operating through you, you know ahead of time what God is going to do." The main thing is whether God gets the glory and whether it brings deliverance to people. In the days in which we are living, there are going to be things happening in the Spirit that are going to absolutely startle us. But the work of God will be done and the name of Jesus will be glorified.

I am excited about the day in which we live because we, the Church, are going to have to be bold enough to claim the workings of the Spirit and go endow the gifts to the needy masses in their spiritual and physical suffering. As we do this, we will find that Christ is just as ready now as He was in His day to confirm His Word with signs following. The Holy Spirit will accommodate you when you are bold enough to claim that which is yours. We are equipped with the Holy Spirit to get the job done, but we have to claim those endowments which God has given unto us and operate in them.

Conclusion

Every day we need to remember the benefits of having the Holy Spirit dwell inside us. He is our Comforter, Helper, Intercessor, Advocate, Strengthener and Standby. He is the Spirit of Truth.

He is a well of living water bubbling up inside us for us to drink from so that we will never have to thirst for the things of God. He works inside us the very nature of Jesus: the fruits of love, joy, peace, longsuffering, gentleness, goodness, faith, meekness and temperance.

We need to remember God's benefits: He is our Healer and our Redeemer. He cleanses us and gives us new life in right standing with Him. We need to renew our minds to the knowledge of the blessings and benefits of having the Spirit of God live inside of us. We need to read the Word of God and build ourselves up by praying in the Spirit daily to learn the ways of the Holy Spirit and His voice.

With the Holy Spirit living inside us, we can intercede for the salvation, healing and deliverance of other people. And moved with the compassion of God, we can reach out and let the gifts of the Spirit manifest through us to pour out and bless others' lives.

We need to learn more about the Holy Spirit for Him to help us and for us to let Him follow through in the call that

He has placed on us. And we have to be established in the difference between the indwelling and outpouring. When we live a life full of the Holy Spirit, He will flow out of us to bless others.

I hope this book has answered any questions you had about learning the ways of the Holy Spirit that will enable you to live in HIS holiness and power. I pray that you will walk in His fullness every day of your life.

Father, I thank You that Your Word has been spoken forth by the Spirit of God through this book. I thank you that as a result, Your Word shall be a part of our lives. It shall not slip from us, and we shall maintain that Word and the understanding which you have given unto us as we *do* the Word with wisdom. Hallelujah!

Father, I pray for each reader of this book to be refreshed in their spirit, soul and body. I thank you for the Word of God which is coming forth and for knowledge and understanding so that each may go forth and *be* the Church that God has called us to be. Energize us with Your Spirit. Lift us up that Your might shall be seen in us, and we shall come forth with a boldness to be *doers* of the Word and not hearers only. May all that is done be for your glory. In Jesus' name. Amen.

Notes

Chapter 9

[1] R. A. Torrey, *The Person and Work of the Holy Spirit* (Grand Rapids: Zondervan, 1974), p. 111.

Chapter 13

[1] James Strong, *The Exhaustive Concordance of the Bible* (Nashville: Abington, 1890), ÒThe Greek Dictionary of the New Testament,Ó p. 57, #4012 and W. E. Vine, *An Expository Dictionary of the New Testament Words,* vol. 2 (Old Tappan: Fleming H. Revell, 1940), p. 147.

[2] Strong, p. 24, #1431

[3] Strong, p. 24, #1435

[4] Strong, p. 47, #3311

[5] Strong, p. 77, #5486

[6] *Webster's New World Dictionary,* 3d college ed., s.v. "prophesy."

To contact Pat Harrison,
write:

Pat Harrison
P. O. Box 35443
Tulsa, OK 74153

*Please include your prayer requests
and comments when you write.*

Additional copies of *Overflowing with the Holy Spirit*,
and *Woman, Wife, Mother* are available from
your local bookstore or by writing:

HARRISON HOUSE
P.O. Box 35035
Tulsa, OK 74153

Pat Harrison is Co-founder and President of Faith Christian Fellowship International in Tulsa, Oklahoma. In 1977, the Lord spoke to Pat and her husband, Buddy, to return to Tulsa to "start a family church, a charismatic training center, and reach the world." Since the first service in January 1978, the outreach of Faith Christian Fellowship has gone beyond Tulsa to touch the entire world.

Today, through FCF's ministerial credentials program, church and traveling ministry programs, and missions outreaches, Pat and her husband oversee 2,000 credentialed ministers and 1,000 churches in the United States and around the world. Since 1980, Pat and Buddy have been "a pastor to pastors and a minister to ministers." Many ministers call her "mom" because she has "mothered" them in the things of God.

Pat and Buddy are particularly noted for operating together in the supernatural ministry of the Holy Spirit, in tongues and interpretation of tongues. Their example of team teaching and flowing in the Holy Spirit together has encouraged other couples in the ministry to do likewise.

Pat has ministered in churches, conventions, women's conferences, and leadership training conferences around the world. Her anointed teaching on the Holy Spirit and on the love of God has influenced Christians on every continent. Thousands have been encouraged to stand in faith and believe God to work miracles in their lives because they have watched Pat persevere in the faith and contend for all that God has said in His Word that she could be and have.

In 1996 the Lord instructed Pat and Buddy to begin another church in Tulsa. The first church established in

1978 is known as the "mother" church. God told the Harrisons that He wanted a "father" church in Tulsa. In obedience to the Lord, they began Father's House in 1997.

In addition to traveling and ministering, Pat has written three books: *Woman, Wife and Mother; Overflowing In The Gifts of the Spirit;* and *How to Raise Your Children in Troubled Times* (co-authored with her husband, Buddy Harrison).